# Your Story Matters

**Your Story Matters: Every Heart Has A Story to Tell**

**Copyright © 2015 | Bridging the Gap**

**ISBN-13: 978-1517387457 | ISBN-10: 1517387450**

Publishing and Design Services | MelindaMartin.me

# Your Story Matters

## EVERY HEART HAS A STORY TO TELL

*Bridging* THE *Gap*

# CONTENTS

To encourage,
equip, and empower
every woman on her
faith journey
with Jesus Christ.

# INTRODUCTION

## Carol Lund, Director of Bridging the Gap

I believe more than anything else that there is a significant calling and purpose for each of us. God has intricately and wonderfully created you. He is mindful of every step you take, every burden you shoulder, every dream you cherish, and every tear you shed. He oversees and orchestrates your life's opportunities to reveal his heart to you. Your story matters to him!

As director of Bridging the Gap, I fully believe our vision statement: "To encourage, equip, and empower every woman on her faith journey with Jesus Christ." Although your journey has individual importance, it is also significant to the whole story. After all, we are in the adventure of life together.

Through life's complexities, God reveals the story of himself. Through him, we have the potential to live out our purpose and impact the world through our stories.

Join us as we consider our individual and corporate importance, influence, and power in understanding our part in God's story. Your story matters because every heart has a story to tell!

It's a beautiful thing when women say yes to God.

# WILL YOU SHARE YOUR STORY?

## Lysa TerKeurst

*"You intended to harm me, but God intended it for good to accomplish what is now being done, the saving of many lives."*

*Genesis 50:20 (NIV)*

Whenever I've stepped out to do something I felt God calling me to do, the voices of criticism and condemnation have been there to greet me. Early on in ministry the voices were loud and cruel. "You'll never be a speaker." "You are not wanted." "Look at you. Do you really think God could use someone like you?"

Sometimes I measured myself against other people. "She's so clever. She's so educated. She's so connected. Who am I compared to all that?" Gradually, I shrank back. I pulled away. I put up a front of perfection with carefully crafted words and a house and kids that looked just right.

Polished on the outside, yet completely undone on the inside.

Eventually the Lord called my bluff. I was simultaneously going through the books *Experiencing God* by Henry Blackaby and *Victory Over the Darkness* by Neil Anderson. Often tears streamed from my eyes while attempting to get through the lessons. But one day it was more than just tears. It was sobs pouring from a chest so heavy with burdens I thought I might literally break apart.

Down on my face, I asked God to speak to me. What I heard in reply was one simple, life-changing question: *Will you share your story?*

"Yes, I will share my story. The good parts that are safe and tidy and acceptable."

But safe and tidy and acceptable were not what God was looking for. He wanted the impossible. Absolutely impossible … in my strength.

God met every one of my arguments with scriptures about relying not on my strength, but on his.

He untangled my need for approval with the challenge to live for an audience of One. He helped me see where the voices of doubt were coming from and challenged me to consider the source. And, quite simply, God kept whispering he loved me over and over again.

The first time I shared my story was an act of absolute obedience. I kept my head down and my guard up. I expected the ladies listening to stone me … especially when I got to the part about my abortion. The shame of childhood abuse and rejection was nothing compared to the shame of my choice to abort my child.

I'd wept over that choice.

I'd repented.

I'd gone to God hundreds of times and asked for forgiveness.

I'd laid it down every time there was an altar call.

But nothing brought the redemption that day brought. As I shook at that podium, I shared exactly what God asked me to.

And then the miracle happened.

When I finished and dared to look up, tear-stained faces were looking back at me. Mouths were whispering, "Me too. Me too."

In that moment, I finally understood the meaning behind Genesis 50:20, *"You intended to harm me, but God intended it for good to accomplish what is now being done, the saving of many lives."*

Seeing God use the very thing that made me feel utterly worthless to help others changed everything. I was finally breaking free from Satan's chains of shame and could see his lies for what they were. In that moment, I felt victorious—not in my own power, but in the Lord's strength and ability to use all things for good.

My saying yes to God gave others the courage to say yes to him as well. Burdens were lifted. Lives were changed. Hidden secrets were touched by grace. It's a beautiful thing when women say yes to God. In what way is he calling you to say yes?

*Lysa TerKeurst is a New York Times best-selling author and president of Proverbs 31 Ministries. Connect with her at www.LysaTerKeurst.com.*

Adapted from: WHAT HAPPENS WHEN WOMEN SAY YES TO GOD DEVOTIONAL
Copyright © 2013 by Lysa TerKeurst
Published by Harvest House Publishers
Eugene, Oregon 97402
www.harvesthousepublishers.com
Used by Permission.

# REFLECT AND RESPOND

In what way is God calling you to say yes to him?

_____

_____

_____

_____

What has God placed on your heart to share with others? Maybe it's your testimony or maybe it's just an encouraging word a friend needs to hear.

_____

_____

_____

_____

# CHOOSING FAITH OVER FEAR

## Jennie Allen

*"If I were still trying to please men, I would not be a servant of Christ."*

*Galatians 1:10 (ESV)*

Over the years, I've received countless emails in my inbox from you. I am overwhelmed by the number of women that have clear dreams but are afraid to pursue them. My husband Zac made an interesting comment when I was discussing this with him. He casually said, "Men don't know what their dreams are and women know, they are just afraid."

I had to agree with him, at least on his point about women. I think we are pretty intuitive and therefore aware of needs around us, aware of the Spirit, and aware of ourselves. We analyze ourselves constantly. So what then is paralyzing so many of us from acting?

I know what it was for me. Fear. I refused to sacrifice the idol of people's opinions. I was so afraid of the invisible thoughts of people.

# Me? You want me?

Last night I sat with one of those friends, wrestling through the tension of the call on her life and what people will think. Her fear is that she would appear self-promoting. Oh! I get that. That was mine, too. So I did nothing.

As if all of this had anything to do with us. As if our reputation mattered enough to sit on our gifts, training, and dreams that could actually help people and make God bigger.

The enemy is subtle and warps truths into lies for us. He tells us we are being humble, responsible, and selfless while we are killing the thing God put us on the planet to do that would build his kingdom.

I think of Moses when God asked him to go and help his people. God said, *My people are in bondage and I want to take them to the land flowing with milk and honey.*

And all Moses heard was "Me? You want me?" As if anything God was doing had a thing to do with him. God was going to do it all, and it was for his people suffering in bondage. But Moses could not get over himself! Thankfully, God used him anyway.

*More from author, teacher, and IF:Gathering founder Jennie Allen can be found at jennieallen.com. This article has been adapted and is used with permission.*

# REFLECT AND RESPOND

What's holding you back?!

_____

_____

_____

_____

What is your anchor? Life's short. Pull up your anchor and sail on, friend.

_____

_____

_____

_____

My God was there.
He sat with me for
hours in the stillness
as I waited for my
body to improve.

# A GIRL AND HER GOD

## Jolene Erlacher

*"In the morning, while it was still very dark, [Jesus] got up and went out to a deserted place, and there he prayed."*

*Mark 1:35 (NRSV)*

It was a small, bright blue room, really more of a closet. In that old church building, where a small group of new believers met in rural Wisconsin, it served as a Sunday school room. I remember as a 5-year-old hearing a story in that little room and knowing one day I would be a missionary. A couple years later, God uprooted my family from a dairy farm and moved us to Mexico, where my parents have now served as missionaries for three decades. We embraced the move and opportunity as the grand adventure with God that it was!

A number of months after arriving in Mexico, I began to develop difficulty breathing. Within a year, it was full-fledged asthma. The air quality where we lived triggered ten years of ongoing breathing issues for me. At first, when I would wake in the night gulping for air, I would run to my parents' room for comfort, help, and prayer. It soon became obvious to me, though, that there was little they could do and depriving them of sleep was pointless. So began a pattern of one little girl's late-night encounters with her God.

As a nine-, ten-, eleven-year-old, I would wake up frequently, wondering if my little lungs would manage to keep me alive until morning. So as to not disturb my sisters, I would sneak out to the hallway or curl up in the living room. There, in the dark stillness, I would cry out to God. At first, my prayers were centered on my fear and struggle to breathe. Eventually, I learned that there was more to discuss with God in those middle-of-the-night sessions. I began to worship, ask questions, pray longer prayers, and expect real answers. I would wake up struggling to breathe and know that God was waiting to meet with me. So we met. As I finished elementary school, navigated middle school, and grew through high school, those meetings with God became my anchor. Then, my senior year, God miraculously touched my body. I could breathe again. I was in the same house, the same town, doing the same things, but I could breathe. I began to realize that asthma had been a gift. Under what other conditions would a child have spent hours and hours seeking, praying, and listening to her God? What I learned through those years of late night encounters with God became a foundation for the rest of my life.

Next came college in America. I am often asked what was hardest about being a missionary kid. That is easy: coming back to America. I remember sitting in the cafeteria at my college in downtown Minneapolis, listening to my peers and thinking, "They are speaking in English, but I have no idea what they are talking about." Culture shock, homesickness, and loneliness engulfed me. I suffered from insomnia. Sharing a room with five other college women provided little privacy. So, late at night, I once more found myself leaving my room. I found a dark closet down the hall that became my sanctuary. There, I would kneel and sing over and over, "I just want to be where You are." God heard me, and once more he met his daughter in the dark stillness. Those closet meetings became my sanity and strength. During those night hours, I learned lessons that could never be taught in theology classes, discipleship groups, or from the chapel platform. I experienced the intimacy of a relational God who had first called me to serve him as a little girl sitting in that blue Sunday school room. My faith deepened in a God who is faithful to walk with us through every season of life.

After graduation, I started working on staff at a church plant. It was an exciting, and often all-consuming, season of life. One day, on my way to the church office, a semi-truck lost control on the snowy interstate. It slid through the median and onto the road in front of me. I hit it head-on going about 60 mph. My car was totaled. I remember the surreal feeling of opening my eyes and touching my legs to be sure I could still feel them. I miraculously walked away from the accident, but not unscathed. The first couple of years after the accident, I lived in denial of the chronic pain in my neck, back, and arms. I frequently panicked at the inability to achieve a waking moment without pain. The thought of a lifetime of chronic pain was crushing. As doctor after doctor, treatment after treatment resulted in managing but never relieving the pain, I began to accept a new reality in my life. Once more, I was waking up in the night, in pain, but surrounded by the presence of my faithful God. He waited for me, longed for time with me, and once more we cherished our late-night dates.

It has been twelve years since that accident, and I still live in chronic pain. Just two weeks ago I was back in the ER, unable to move from the severity of the pain. Three days in bed, as friends and family helped care for my two-year-old twins, was humbling.

But guess what? My God was there. He sat with me for hours in the stillness as I waited for my body to improve.

Do I pray and hope for the day when God alleviates my pain the way he touched my lungs and my loneliness in former seasons? Of course. Yet, I have come to learn that my God is jealous for me. He can use anything in my life, when surrendered to him, for a greater purpose. I can stand here today, over 30 years removed from that little blue classroom, and say that I am a girl who is madly in love with her God and desires to be used by him. I am so thankful for his drawing me to him through every season of life. I wouldn't change a thing. The pain of the past is just that—past. The pain of today is temporary. My relationship with him is eternal, and his grace, faithfulness, and glory make the future bright indeed!

# REFLECT AND RESPOND

Is there a challenging piece of your story in which God is waiting to meet you?

_____

_____

_____

_____

How will you respond?

_____

_____

_____

_____

Unrealistic
expectations can be so
harmful in
the waiting process.

# SEASONS OF WAITING

## Carolyn Haas

*"But those who wait on the Lord*
*Shall renew their strength;*
*They shall mount up with wings like eagles,*
*They shall run and not be weary,*
*They shall walk and not faint."*

*Isaiah 40:31 (NKJV)*

I love Amazon Prime because I am guaranteed free 2-day shipping. It's an amazing, on-demand world we live in with smartphones, apps, and online streaming. Fast shipping is great because, let's face it, none of us like to wait. I mean, doesn't a yellow traffic light translate as "quick, speed up!" rather than "slow down and wait"? Yet the longer I've navigated life, leadership, and ministry, the more I see the importance of learning how to wait.

My husband Peter and I planted Substance Church almost 11 years ago in Minneapolis, Minn. As church planters and leaders, we have always had a huge vision in our heart. If I can be honest, however, it's always surprised me to watch how long it has taken for parts of the vision to be seen and walked out. Like all church planters, we have tried to get a permanent facility. I'm excited to say that we are finally renovating our first facility and should be moved in by January 2016. But if the Lord had told me seven years ago that it would take this long for us to get a facility, I would have wept. In all honesty, while I can now see that God's timing for us and Substance is perfect, the last few years as we cast vision, searched for land/properties, and raised funds for an ambiguous location, it was so discouraging having door after door closed shut.

Although I can see now that God was doing a deep, beautiful work in our hearts, I first had to learn a few lessons in the trenches of waiting.

During seasons of waiting, it's easy to get insecure and think that if I was a better leader, employee, friend, wife, or mom, then maybe I wouldn't be in this holding pattern—maybe I could actually make something happen sooner. And unfortunately, the world is full of "Job's friends" who affirm our insecurities by telling us what we need to do to get beyond the particular season we find ourselves in. I've also felt misunderstood, like people were looking at my life and wondering why "fill in the blank" wasn't happening. To be honest, so was I. Unrealistic expectations can be so harmful in the waiting process.

I've found that in seasons of waiting and uncertainty, it's easy to form our own theology about what God can or can't do or will or won't do. We tend to look at our current experience and form our own beliefs rather than looking to God and his Word, which never changes. Yet waiting reveals who or what we trust. Do we lean on our own understanding or do we fully trust in the Lord (Proverbs 3:5-6)? Recently I heard Christine Caine talk about how when we wait upon the Lord we will renew our strength (Isaiah 40:31), but so many times we are waiting on the wrong thing—which is evident by our lack of strength. And because seasons of waiting have unknown timelines, it's easy to become tired.

In human pregnancy, we know that the gestational period is nine months. But when it comes to what God is birthing and forming in us, the gestational period isn't always clear. If you talk to any woman who is 39 weeks pregnant, the number one question she gets asked is, "When are you due?" It gets to the point where she doesn't even want to go out in public because it's so annoying to be asked questions about something over which she has no control.

At least with pregnancy, we know the baby will eventually come out (most health professionals won't allow you to go past 42 weeks), but for most life events there is no official "due date." It's much more difficult to answer questions like, "Why aren't you married?" "When are you having kids?" "Why aren't you healed?" "Why don't you have a church building yet?" It's easy to get frustrated and insecure.

Yet when we look at biblical precedent and the faith stories of the cloud of witnesses who have gone before us, we see a pattern of waiting:

- Abraham and Sarah waited 20 years before their dream came true.

- Moses waited 40 years before he became a leader.

- David spent years in the wilderness exiled and on the run before he became king.

- Jesus waited 30 years before his "ministry" opportunities became public.

I don't know what you are waiting for today. But let me encourage you with this: God sees and hears (Genesis 16). He knows (1 Samuel 2). He has a plan (Jeremiah 29:11). And when those insecurities, uncertainties, fears, and anxieties try to mess with your thoughts and emotions, just take a deep breath and realize it's a sign that you need to run to the One who loves you and knows you. When you know you have a good Father "who knows what you need before you even ask" (Matthew 6), you can rest assured that "your times are in his hands" (Psalm 31:15).

# REFLECT AND RESPOND

What if you engaged today as an opportunity to rest in God's love rather than to dwell on what is not yet at hand?

_____

_____

_____

_____

What is God revealing about himself to you in this season?

_____

_____

_____

_____

What can you be thankful for in this season of waiting?

_____

_____

_____

_____

# THE MOST SPECTACULAR STORY ON EARTH

## Jen Spiegel

*"Now it's time to change your ways! Turn to face God so he can wipe away your sins, pour out showers of blessing to refresh you, and send you the Messiah he prepared for you."*

*Acts 3:19 (MSG)*

Come close, friends. I have a secret I'm about to share with you. It's a little odd, I realize, but in sharing our stories, we all have quirks that come out sooner or later, right? Well, here it is: I am obsessed with the circus. Now, before your judge-o-meter starts leaning dangerously into the red "weirdo" zone, please know that I don't mean the sad circus situation of the present day, with mullet-hair-rocking, leather-pants-wearing men riding motorcycles in a spherical cage before heading out back for a smoke. Also, there are exactly zero creepy clown dolls in my house.

I mean the kind of circus that rolled silently into town while everyone was sleeping and magically appeared at the break of dawn, bringing wonder and excitement to big cities and small towns across the country, the train circus that lived its glory days during the early 20th century. The thing I love about circus history is that it is packed with stories. Some are true. Some are legends. Some are straight up smoke and mirrors. Glitzy, dark, mysterious, dangerous. It all just sucks me in. But the story of the incredible life of Mabel Stark has perhaps drawn me in more than any other.

Mabel's early life, like that of many circus figures, is a bit of a mystery. Born in Kentucky around 1889, Mabel grew up with a dream of working with animals, although after her parents died, practicality led her to nursing school. After graduating in 1911, she serendipitously met a circus manager who offered her a job training goats and horses. Mabel saw her chance to make her childhood dreams a reality and traded her white nurse's uniform for sequins and short skirts in a heartbeat.

But Mabel's passion didn't lie with riding horses around a ring. Although nearly unheard of for a woman in her day, she wanted to work with tigers, and she didn't stop until she reached her dream. By around 1915, Mabel, having exchanged her sequins for head-to-toe leather, was making gentlemen scream and ladies swoon with her seemingly effortless command of up to 12 tigers at a time, sometimes throwing a lion or panther into the steel cage for good measure.

Magazines promoted her. Photographers couldn't get close enough. People loved her. Under the big top, in the center of a hushed crowd, Mabel must have looked incredible. Beautiful, talented, brave, the envy of all. Her life must have looked spectacular.

But when the tigers were tucked away for the night and the train rolled on to the next town, life wasn't always as bright as it seemed. Mabel's personal life included between four and six marriages, all but one of which she later claimed were simply attempts to further her career. Mabel occasionally kept tigers in her apartment and even took them for walks along Venice Beach in the off-season, but the animals she loved so much nearly took her life on many occasions. Crushed bones, countless lacerations, and a nearly severed arm and leg requiring over 700 stitches were just some of the injuries Mabel suffered throughout her career.

Yet she never wavered in her love for the magnificent, striped creatures. Mabel recognized her passion and lived it with abandon.

Beautiful, talented, brave, the envy of all. Her life must have looked spectacular.

In her autobiography, *Hold That Tiger*, Mabel wrote, "Mine may seem a strange profession…I have been clawed and slashed and chewed until there is hardly an inch of my body unscarred by tooth or nail. But I love these big cats as a mother loves her children."

And yet despite finding her life's passion, the ending of Mabel's story is not a happy one. As the great circuses fell to bankruptcy one by one, Mabel found herself floundering for meaning without her giant furry companions. In 1968, at the age of 79, she wrote a letter, swallowed a handful of pills, and never woke up.

I have often wondered what went wrong for Mabel, why she couldn't look back on her fantastic 60-year career with satisfaction. But the more time passes, the more I realize how quickly life just slips away, often taking our aspirations and treasures with it. And Mabel must have thought, *All that work, all these scars, and what of it?*

What we believe about our story? It matters. A lot.

Without the belief in a God who can redeem all we experience, who can take our small failures, our gigantic screw-ups, and all the things out of our control, and turn them into good for us and those around us, life feels a bit like wandering through a cage full of tigers, wondering which one is going to take a bite out of us next.

Even with God by our side, life will scar us. But when we stop dragging our pain and disappointment around with us, when we lay it at his feet and say, *Take it, Lord. Make it good. And make it matter,* he will. He will.

When we give it all to him, God will use absolutely every chapter of our stories to teach, to heal, and to redeem.

The most spectacular story on Earth is the one God is writing—a phrase, a sentence, a paragraph at a time—in each of our lives. Without the words he is writing in your life, the story is less than complete.

Mabel's story mattered. She just didn't know it.

Connecting our story to God's story: This is where the pieces of life that seem so fleeting find a permanent home. This is where the tigers' teeth get removed from our flesh. This is where a story is transformed from scarred to spectacular.

# REFLECT AND RESPOND

Are there pieces of your story you need to turn over to God?

_____

_____

_____

_____

How might the tough parts of your story fit into God's story, even today?

_____

_____

_____

_____

I never imagined
that one of the
keys to my freedom
was something
I had all along.

# FORGIVENESS AND THE PEAR-SHAPED MAN

## Sarah Kallies

*"Love your enemies, do good to those who hate you."*

*Luke 6:27 (NIV)*

I was 19 years old, and there wasn't a cloud in sight as I lay, eyes closed, music flowing from my headphones. It was a sunny day on the bluffs overlooking the Mississippi River when the first of two tiny pebbles fell on my stomach. Alert now, my eyes followed the line of bushes at my back. I checked my watch. *I'll only stay five more minutes.*

Suddenly, a dark cloud seemed to cover the whole earth. As my eyes adjusted, I began to make out the shadow of a man over the top of me. The devil, adorned in nothing but a nylon mask, had come.

*Where are his clothes?*

*His body is shaped like a pear.*

*I wonder if the people across the river can see this?*

The amount of absurd thoughts that can go through a person's mind at the most inopportune moments is amazing.

In between these misfires of thought I tried to get up, but his hands were already on me, in places they did not belong. And I finally understood what the term "out-of-body experience" meant. It was the stuff of bad made-for-TV movies. When my screams were heard by nearby hikers, he ran. And like any good American, or misguided female in a horror film (the scenes we all roll our eyes at), I chased him.

With the full force of my 100-pound frame, I knocked him down and saw his neatly folded clothes on the ground nearby. It was then I knew that I needed to get away or I might die. So I ran. My brain was firing away, but my legs stopped working as I tripped my way up to the road. As the police, the fire personnel, and search dog showed up, I reassured myself, "This isn't actually happening."

Months later at a police lineup, all I could say was, "Why am I alive? Why did I chase him?" I felt I had done everything wrong.

The detective responded simply yet forcefully, "Sarah, you did everything right. You survived."

Maybe I had been hit one too many times as a child. Maybe in trying to destroy me in my younger years, the devil had inadvertently created a seasoned fighter. What was certain was that this man had stalked the wrong girl. I was not silent or compliant. Most who are do not survive. Yet I did not feel worthy of living.

Later, when I was at the bottom of a bottle, or laid out on the bathroom floor full of pills, or waking up in a different guy's bed. When bitterness turned into an inability to maintain friendships or even leave my apartment. When trying to kill myself a year later was just one more thing I failed at...

God whispered truth:

*I mattered.*

*I had purpose.*

*I had survived.*

It would be nearly 15 years before I hit rock bottom and finally began to surrender. I never imagined that one of the keys to my freedom was something I had all along.

Forgiveness.

Forgiveness for myself. Forgiveness for the pear-shaped man. So much so that I look forward to a day when I hope to see my attacker in Glory and know that, in this case, the devil did not win.

I started to pray for my attacker because, contrary to popular belief, forgiveness is not actually about the offender. It's about you. Your decision regarding what to do with the hurt. Will you wear it like a bad hairdo? Allow it to change you into a lesser person? Or will you release it, taking away its power?

Every time we choose to hang on to a hurt, we are knowingly choosing to own it. And darkness wins. Instead, we should be reserving that priceless room in our lives for the things that truly matter.

Imagine what our lives would be like if Jesus whipped out our failings whenever he felt like it. We're sitting in church and suddenly the pastor points at us, asks us to stand up, and calls us out on that secret affair or addiction in front of everyone. Hello.

Jesus set the standard in death. God declared our sins "as far as the east is from the west" (Psalm 103:12) and "on the bottom of the ocean floor" (Micah 7:19).

It takes time. In some cases, depending on the severity of the wrong, it may take years of consistently repeating to yourself and to God that even if your heart doesn't feel it yet, you choose forgiveness.

# REFLECT AND RESPOND

Who do you need to forgive today?

_____

_____

_____

_____

What hurt have you been holding onto? You've let it own a part of you it shouldn't. Let today be the day you let the light come in and shine where, for too long, it has been dark.

_____

_____

_____

_____

# A FEARFUL YES

## Kendra Roehl

*"But the Lord said to Samuel, '...The Lord does not look at the things people look at. People look at the outward appearance, but the Lord looks at the heart.' "*

*1 Samuel 16:7 (NLT)*

I sit in the front row, my Bible in my lap. Palms sweating and heart racing, it takes everything in me not to run from the room. I wait as the clock slowly ticks by, anxiously anticipating my turn to read a short passage of scripture that I'd practiced more times than I could count. My turn comes. I stand behind the podium to read, too quiet for anyone to hear, looking only at the text, everyone else a blur, then hurriedly sit back down.

I've always had fear. And fear of public speaking was at the top of the list. In college when everyone was required to take speech class, I dropped the first section I was in when the professor told us we'd be giving *three* speeches in class. I was too freaked out to think about getting up in front of others. I searched until I found a professor who only required her students to get up twice.

But even with all this erratic fear, inside, I have always felt like speaking was something God placed in my heart to do. This crazy whisper of an idea, never shared with anyone, too unrealistic to me to ever be realized or even verbalized. Or so I thought.

But as the years went on and my faith continued to grow, I began to trust God's direction. Little by little, small step after small step, I began to trust where he was leading. An announcement during service, a prayer spoken at Bible study, emceeing a women's event, giving the message one night during youth group.

All leading up to today. Sometimes I can't believe that I am this person—part of the speaking team at my church, regularly sharing at women's groups in my area, and blogging about life and faith for Bridging the Gap.

# Maybe it's time to start letting God be big in our lives.

It makes me stand in awe of God. And what he can accomplish through his people.

Because if you went back and talked to anyone from my childhood or early 20s, they would be surprised to hear what I'm doing. There was nothing about my outward personality that lined up with the title of "speaker." There was nothing external that would make people think this was my gifting. If anything, on the outside, it looked like the exact opposite.

But God has reminded others in the Bible not to look at the outward appearance, and it's a lesson we can continue to learn from today.

That flicker of a dream you have in your heart? That gifting or calling you sense in your spirit, but are too timid to pursue? What if all these things are from God?

What if all he's waiting for is your ability to trust him to accomplish what he has planned?

Maybe it's time to start letting God be *big* in our lives. Maybe it's time to say *yes* to his plan.

Maybe it's time to claim his promises of love and grace, mercy and provision for ourselves and not just other people.

Maybe it's time to let God be God.

# REFLECT AND RESPOND

What part of your story—that part that's still just a dream—is God just waiting to write?

_____

_____

_____

_____

# COUNTING ON GOD

## Lisa Demuth

*"But if...you seek the Lord your God, you will find him
if you seek him with all your heart and with all your soul."*

*Deuteronomy 4:29 (NIV)*

After a morning filled with bike rides, sidewalk chalk art, and multiple times up and down the slide, it was finally time for lunch. As we sat down to eat, my question of who would like to pray was enthusiastically answered by my four-year-old grandson.

He began, "Dear God, thank you for today. Help us have a good day; no crabby kids. We love you, God; we love everybody. We're counting on you, God. Amen."

Both of my grandboys, ages three and four, have prayed the "no crabby kids" part before. (It gets me every time!) But the "we're counting on you" part was new. I wondered: *Did he hear his parents pray this way? Did he hear it in church?* I pondered those words, "We're counting on you, God," throughout the day, not realizing the important role they were about to play over the next days and weeks for our family.

Shortly after that day with my grandboys, my husband and I took our youngest son in for a followup visit with his doctor. This scheduled appointment quickly turned into an unexpected hospitalization lasting 18 days. During that time, numerous medical interventions were tried, yet they all failed. The last option was a very invasive surgery that would change our son's life, but it was potentially the cure that was so desperately needed.

We sought God as never before. We prayed for healing. We searched scripture and were comforted by words of truth. We received encouragement from family and friends.

Throughout this time, we were counting on God. We were counting on God for healing. We were counting on God for wisdom. We were counting on God for direction. We were counting on God for peace. I continued to hear the simple prayer declared by my grandson in his sweet four-year-old voice. "We're counting on you, God."

Our prayer for healing for our son was answered. God worked through the surgical team that he had gifted. The first of three major surgeries has been completed. Our son is disease-free!

Walking through this medical crisis with our son has been one of the hardest things that we, as parents, have experienced. It was unexpected and caught us off-guard. Yet, it shouldn't come as a surprise when we face difficult times. John 16:33 says, "In this world you will have trouble" (NIV).

But no matter how hard things become, we can take comfort in knowing that God has promised that he will never leave us! Isaiah 43:1-3 says, "Do not fear, for I have redeemed you; I have summoned you by name; you are Mine. When you pass through the waters, I will be with you; and when you pass through the rivers, they will not sweep over you. When you walk through the fire, you will not be burned...For I am the Lord, your God, the Holy One of Israel, your Savior" (NIV).

When is seems as if my strength is gone, I am also comforted by Deuteronomy 31:6: "Be strong and courageous. Do not be afraid or terrified...for the Lord your God goes with you; he will never leave you nor forsake you" (NIV).

# We're counting on you, God.

Counting on God during hard times comes naturally for me. But what about counting on God during the good times? Am I counting on God by seeking his direction and expectantly looking for his answer, or are my prayers more about me "sharing" my plans with God and asking him to bless them? I want to count on God during the good times with the same intensity as I count on him during the hard times.

# REFLECT AND RESPOND

Do you count on God during the good times as well as during the hard times?

_____

_____

_____

_____

Can you think of a time in your life when you know that God was with you? In what way will you count on God today?

_____

_____

_____

_____

# SAYING YES TO RIGHT NOW

## Kristin Demery

*"I've learned by now to be quite content whatever my circumstances. I'm just as happy with little as with much, with much as with little. I've found the recipe for being happy whether full or hungry, hands full or hands empty. Whatever I have, wherever I am, I can make it through anything in the One who makes me who I am."*

*Philippians 4:11-13 (MSG)*

I lost my mind at 2 p.m. on a Friday. We were on a ferryboat ride to Fort Sumter, South Carolina, and the combination of two days' worth of flights and long car rides, no naps for our young children, and abbreviated bedtimes had worn us all a bit thin.

The kids were whiny, but I was determined to paste a smile on my face for the sake of my husband's family. As Tim got up to bring 3-year-old Noelle to the bathroom at the back of the ferry, my forced cheer dissipated as things went from bad to worse between 5-year-old Elise and me.

"I want a granola bar!" she said loudly, attracting the attention of those sandwiched into the undersized seats surrounding us.

"No, honey, you just had a banana," I remonstrated quietly. "You can have one in a little bit."

"I WANT A GRANOLA BAR!" she hollered, her voice rising an octave as she started thrashing in her chair, legs kicking out.

"No," I said, grabbing her little arm with a strong grip, "And that's *not* how you talk to Mama."

And with that, I promptly burst into tears. Shuffling in my bag, I quickly grabbed a pair of sunglasses, shoving them on my nose to mask my embarrassment. I'm sure my celebrity sunglasses routine fooled no one, but I didn't want anyone's sympathy, pity, or judgment.

Sensing my distress, my husband's stepmother moved from across the aisle to turn her sweet Southern charm on my recalcitrant preschooler. Eventually, Elise was distracted from her desire to have another snack, and I outwardly pulled myself together. But inside the misery remained.

*What's wrong with me?* I wondered, feeling helpless in the face of my strong-willed child.

## I've learned by now to be quite content whatever my circumstances.

I've heard it said—usually by people who mean well, people whose children are long grown and gone from the house—that when it comes to young children, "the days are long, but the years are short." I think that's probably true, but there are times when I find myself struggling to see beyond the next hour or two, much less a full day. The reality is, I am a mom of three children under the age of six. I guzzle two cups of coffee before 8 a.m. I don't care if my children actually rest during "rest time"; I just want them to stay upstairs for an hour so I can eat lunch in solitude. I stay up too late reading books on my phone because it's the only time of day that no one is touching or talking to me. I compulsively eat chocolate in the pantry. Some days I snipe at my husband when he's leaving the house for a work or social commitment because I'm jealous.

If I'm honest, sometimes I just have a hard time saying "yes" to my current life. And all too often, my daily circumstances can spiral into negative if/then patterns:

*If I lose my patience, then I cannot expect my children to learn how to be patient themselves.*

*If I don't see other people struggling with their own children, then there must be something wrong with the way I parent.*

*If my children are behaving badly, then I must be a bad mom.*

*And, worst of all: If life feels hard, then it must not be good.*

What gets lost in the middle of all this mess are the little things that really matter. The toothless smiles from a five-month-old who adores her big sisters but hates bottles. The curly-haired three-year-old who calls her dollies "shweetie" and wakes up early to climb into bed with me. And the five-year-old who tells me that she's glad God made her to like pink hearts.

Here's the real truth, the one that gets buried in my stacks of laundry like so many mismatched socks: If I can't find contentment in my current circumstances, then I won't be ready for what God has next. But if I *can* learn how to say yes to right now, then I'll find the contentment I seek and be willing to be used exactly where I'm at—right in the middle of my messy life. Even when life feels hard, it can still be very, very good.

# REFLECT AND RESPOND

What current circumstances in your life do you need to say "yes" to?

_____

_____

_____

_____

What lesson is God teaching you in the messes of your daily life?

_____

_____

_____

_____

# RENEWING YOUR MIND

## Nancy Holte

*"Do not conform to the pattern of this world, but be transformed by the renewing of your mind."*

*Romans 12:2 (NIV)*

Your own parents don't want you, so why do you think we'd want you?" This question played on repeat in Sara's mind for many years. Imagine being in high school and hearing that question from the girl competing against you for a position in a school club. Words—they can pierce like a knife.

Sara's life was filled with pain long before those words were even uttered. When her parents divorced, she was left with an absentee father and a mother who brutally abused and burned her. In the summer of her fifth grade year, her aunt took her to church, where she heard the "hellfire and brimstone" pastor preach, "If you don't believe in Jesus, you'll go to hell." All Sara's little ten-year-old mind could think about was how much pain she felt from cigarette burns inflicted by her mother. She didn't want to hurt forever, so she gave her life to Jesus and was baptized that night. Her relationship with Christ, although founded in a very wounded heart, had begun. The issues of her life remained, but deep down Sara knew God was always there, nudging her closer to him.

It was Sara's high school track coach who noticed her constant burns and called Child Protective Services to look into it. Soon, Sara was moved into the foster care system. By the time she was 16 years old she'd been pregnant twice. It was the late 70s, and Roe vs. Wade had recently allowed women the option to abort. In Sara's case, however, abortion wasn't optional; it was forced upon her by her social worker. The aftermath of the abortions sent Sara into a depression that wouldn't lift until 2007, 30 years later.

Sara's 18th birthday coincided with her high school commencement, and because she had aged out of foster care Sara had nowhere to go. She sought out various family members, hoping there would be someone who could provide her with a home that looked more like the Waltons than hell. When that dream died, she looked for love the only way she knew how to find it—in the arms of men. Once again Sara found herself pregnant, but this time she didn't even entertain the idea of an abortion. She refused to go through the mental pain and anguish of yet another stolen pregnancy.

Sara's desire was to avoid using welfare or food stamps, but she also realized her baby girl needed food to eat, clothes to wear, and a safe place to live. By now Sara was involved with a church, and some of the men in her church (yes, you read that correctly) exchanged time with her to help her pay her bills! Sometimes the men just wanted to go out for dinner, enjoy her companionship, and be seen with a beautiful woman; other times they wanted sex. Sara knew what she was doing was wrong, but by now her self-esteem was buried deep in a pit, and she enjoyed the idea of men wanting to be with her. "It's the only lifestyle I'm worthy of," Sara reasoned.

All along, the words still played in her mind, "Your own parents don't want you, so why do you think we'd want you?"

Eventually Sara married the first man who proposed to her. She didn't love him but again figured it was the best she deserved. The mind can be a terrible liar. Sara's husband turned out to be a drug runner, and Sara regularly indulged in drugs, liquor, and cigarettes. It was after her divorce, Sara said, that she "cleaned up her act a bit."

## I am the image of a perfect God.

The next man she met was an upstanding guy, and when he proposed to her she thought, "Who would ever marry someone like me?" Never feeling worthy of her life, she struggled with depression and threatened suicide on a regular basis. When she looked at her life through her own guilt and pain, she saw herself as wounded, a victim. She had no idea that God saw her as adventurous, creative, loving, and beautiful.

When her marriage of 17 years was falling apart, Sara formed an extensive plan for taking her life. She thought no one would miss her and it would be best for everyone. It was then that she entered the Minirth-Meier (now Meier) Clinic as her last hope. Her divorce papers arrived while she was an inpatient, and when family members refused to visit, she was left feeling abandoned and unworthy.

Sara's therapist at Minirth-Meier gave her one assignment: to look in the mirror every day and say, "I love you."

"I hated it," Sara recalls. But, after 60 days, she looked in the mirror and said, "I love you, and I like you too." That statement surprised her so much that she looked in the mirror again and said, "I really *do* like you!"

In the ensuing months and now years, Sara has learned to see herself through God's eyes as a woman made in his image. She still has times when she hears those old words that pierced her so deeply, but now she has a new tape running in her brain: "I am the image of a perfect God."

Sara hasn't forgotten what it's like to feel those emotions, and she uses that information to help others. She fills her mind with words of life because she knows change comes from the inside out, through a relationship with Christ Jesus. He speaks life!

# REFLECT AND RESPOND

Whose words are you allowing to feed your soul?

_____

_____

_____

_____

One inch at a time,
we made our way
slowly there.

# A MOTHER'S LOVE

## Shari Harris

*"Beloved, let us love one another, for love is from God, and whoever loves has been born of God and knows God. Anyone who does not love does not know God, because God is love."*

*1 John 4:7-8 (ESV)*

Looking back on my childhood, I can really only imagine how often my mom made sacrifices for our family. We grew up on Whitewater Trail in Brooklyn Park, Minn., during the late 60s and early 70s in a modest neighborhood filled with hard-working, middle-class families. Like most children growing up in that era, I was busy flying kites, playing softball, hanging out with my friends, and doing all the things kids do growing up—never giving a thought to how much my mom loved me or if there were any sacrifices being made on my behalf in order to have a childhood that included so many good things.

As an adult, I had the opportunity to really see and appreciate how much my mom loved us and always put her kids before everything else. Through her example, I learned that a mother's unconditional love for her children is second only to God's extraordinary, perfect love for us, his children. I also learned we are only able to love our kids so much because God first loved us. My mother's love is indelibly etched in my heart and soul. I thank God for her example of selfless love, which was never more evident than when she boldly and courageously fought a terminal illness, as ALS slowly ravaged her body, overtaking her ability to function normally.

My mother dealt with the devastating blow of an ALS diagnosis with her head held high, and I think, at least in part, she managed life with a terminal illness and extreme physical challenges so well for the sake of her family. She never wanted us to feel bad for her; she wanted to protect us from hurting and seemed to put this above even her suffering. Even when she couldn't swallow and had to have a tube put into her stomach for nourishment, even as her muscles atrophied to the point of having little use of her limbs, I saw her worrying more about others— especially her kids—than herself.

In the spring of 2010, we went on our last annual opening weekend fishing trip. Her health had rapidly declined that winter, and knowing it was more than likely our last trip with her was hard. She loved to fish. Despite having almost lost the use of her arms and legs, and though barely able to shuffle her legs, with our help, she wasn't going to miss fishing. I'll never forget how long it took her to shuffle down to the dock and into the boat. It was heartbreaking. But she was happy, and we were happy for her.

I had prayed and prayed that she would be able to take that trip, and there she was in the boat. I asked God to let her catch a fish. She did—a little walleye—and her eyes sparkled. At the same time, a tear glistened in my eye, knowing it was going to be the last fish she was going to be able to catch.

Later, when my mom and I were settled back into the cabin and the guys were back on the lake, she wanted to walk to the store. Walking the quarter mile between our cabin and the little country store was an activity we had always done without even thinking about it. But that last year, even with my mom hardly able to walk, much less on the gravel shoulder of a busy road, she still wanted to go. I worried what I would do if something happened along the way. If she fell, I didn't know how I would help her back to her feet. Yet I could not possibly deny her determination to travel the road. One inch at a time, we made our way slowly there. Every year she bought me a little trinket from the country store, and it turns out that was why she was so insistent we take that quarter-mile journey, which felt much more like three miles to me that day. When we finally arrived, she bought me a little bear angel holding a sign that said, "I love you."

Mom's courage and tenacity still amaze and inspire me today. Her body wasn't able to fight off ALS, but she still fought off despair, discouragement, and all the expected trappings of terminal illness. She loved Jesus. She loved her family. And even under extremely difficult circumstances, she taught us that God's love could be trusted.

# REFLECT AND RESPOND

What experiences have you endured that have made you question God's love, his plans, or his faithfulness? Life is hard, but God is good. It's not a trite cliche; it's a truth that I hope you discover in your own life and circumstances.

_____

_____

_____

_____

# TRUST AND TRANSFORMATION

## Andrea Munsch

*"But the Lord stood with me and gave me strength."*

*2 Timothy 4:17 (NLT)*

In January 2015, I took "before" pictures. Looking back at them now, I can clearly see I had stepped outside of God's will for my life, although I wouldn't have labeled it as such at the time. After having my first child and conceiving my second shortly after, I started ignoring what my body and soul needed as I adjusted to life as a stay-at-home mom.

Motherhood hit me like a ton of bricks, buried me in diapers, and I was desperately trying to hold it together. I saw my circumstances, including my emergency C-sections, health problems, and my mother fighting breast cancer, as a reason to treat my body terribly. I felt I didn't have a choice other than to ignore my needs to make it through that stressful time in my life.

From 2011 to 2015 I gained 50 pounds, and the number on the scale kept climbing. Attempting to reverse this seemed nearly impossible, so I began accepting my weight problem by defending it with excuses. I felt paralyzed and unable to begin any of the marketed weight-loss plans and fad diets because I knew I couldn't succeed with those programs. It wasn't possible to change everything about my lifestyle overnight and I didn't know where else to start, so nothing changed.

Years of carrying the extra weight eventually manifested as a new set of health problems. I had migraines, neck and back problems, acid reflux, anxiety and panic attacks, stomach sensitivities, even fatty liver. Every day I was peeling myself off the floor, completely depleted, trying to pour myself out to my family when I had no reserves to draw from.

Over time, the extra weight began looking normal to me. After years of getting comfortable in my yoga pants, I began wearing the 50 pounds of weight gain like a badge of motherhood honor. Even though I wasn't admitting it outwardly, deep down I knew this wasn't who I wanted to be.

In January of 2015, I was at my lowest. I never thought I'd share the photos I took publicly, but I needed them as motivation. I promised myself I would find a way to succeed in losing weight and becoming a healthier person. After making that promise, I refused to go on a diet (because I'd only quit). I refused to set up a regimented workout plan (because I'd only feel governed by it and then quit). I decided to make one small change at a time. And that made all the difference in the world.

I started by removing processed foods from my diet. I took this process slowly, choosing one item at a time. I quickly became thankful for the small triumphs, like getting through a meal without taking two acid-blocking medications. I was seeing changes at a snail's pace, but I was excited about the new journey I had begun. I then educated myself on healthier food choices. I celebrated the new perspective on health I had for my family, even though we were inching our way there. Six months after promising myself things would change, I had lost 47 pounds and never had to conform to a diet or exercise program.

*I decided to make one small change at a time.*

But this battle that began in 2011 wasn't really about the weight. It was realizing I had forgotten about the life God was inviting me to live. I spent years disconnected from God's encouragement, energy, and guidance. Not realizing it at the time, God was taking my hand and guiding me as I fearfully and sometimes reluctantly shuffled through a dark room, just waiting to reach the other side. Instead of removing my pain, God revealed his trustworthiness. God does not waste pain, and he showed this to be true in my journey. In six months, he restored my relationship with him and improved the health of my entire family. Even if you are as broken as I was, God can work in your life, repairing your damages. He can mold you into a new person, with new habits and new joy.

God will always campaign for our hearts and our lives. If we choose to walk the challenging path of transformation with him, we'll realize he's been worthy of our trust the whole time.

# REFLECT AND RESPOND

Are there any pieces of your story God is waiting to transform?

_____

_____

_____

_____

Are you ready to begin that journey with him?

_____

_____

_____

_____

# MORE THAN A RING

## Kristen Ostrem

*"...I came that they may have life, and have it abundantly."*

*John 10:10 (NASB)*

Recently, I was eating dinner with a peer and four young girls. During our time together, I suggested an idea for a scenario in the future when they might be with someone and need a conversation starter. The idea was to ask the significance to the other person's jewelry, as what someone wears oftentimes has a meaningful story involving where it was purchased, why it is worn, or from whom it was received.

One youth was quick to ask for the meaning behind the ring that I wear—a small silver band with a hollowed-out shape of the cross in the middle. I smiled, knowing the symbolism behind my ring, one tied to a monumental moment when God spoke to my heart.

When I was about 17 years old, I was by myself on a training run for an upcoming cross country or track season. As I was running down the road and thinking, I heard God speak these words in the quiet of my heart: "If you ever think anything negative about me, it's simply not true."

Though that particular statement was simple, it laid a foundation from which all other perspectives in my life began to stem from. God's quiet revelation to me was that although the mind, our society, or one's own experiences can create believable understandings about him, those views may not be correct.

You see, even though I grew up in the church, I too had years of difficulty understanding his love for me and struggled not to feel as though my value was partly performance-based. Despite having a loving family, physical health, and other blessings, my perception of God's love has often been based on head knowledge rather than heart knowledge. I've come to realize that in every area of life, there is a battle for our minds between what is true versus what is a lie. John 8:44 says that "...[The devil] was a murderer from the beginning, and does not stand in the truth because there is no truth in him. Whenever he speaks a lie, he speaks from his own nature, for he is a liar and the father of lies" (NASB). Then again in 1 Peter 5:8, we are warned: "Be of sober spirit, be on the alert. Your adversary, the devil, prowls around like a roaring lion, seeking someone to devour" (NASB).

Understanding the struggle means that it is vital to measure our beliefs according to absolute truth, which is the Word of God. Evaluating the way we perceive God is essential because it impacts our trust in him, relationship with him, and ultimately our life lived with him. Many people believe that God is distant, doesn't care, or is uninvolved in their lives. Others believe he is angry at them or that he could never forgive what they have done.

Yet we know that those negative feelings aren't from God. In fact, Jesus said, "This is eternal life, that they may know You, the only true God, and Jesus Christ whom You have sent" (John 17:3,

NASB). Likewise, "The thief comes only to steal and kill and destroy; I came that they may have life, and have it abundantly" (John 10:10, NASB). Because of the foundation laid in my heart through what God spoke to me, I choose to measure my feelings according to truth and believe that he is good, trustworthy, and has abundant life for me to realize! As I continue to seek him, listen for his voice, find ways to be with him, and ask for his Holy Spirit's presence in my life, God continues to reveal himself and his love for me.

For me, my ring is a symbol that God is the truth to base my life upon, and that no matter how I feel, the truth is that he is always good and always loves me.

*If you ever think anything negative about me, it's simply not true.*

# REFLECT AND RESPOND

What does your current view of God look like? Does it reflect the character of God as revealed through his Word, or is it based on external factors like the way you were raised or society's view of him?

_____

_____

_____

_____

How does your view of God influence your daily life?

_____

_____

_____

_____

# THE BEST LEMONADE MAKER

## Tabby Finton

*"And we know that God causes everything to work together for the good of those who love God and are called according to his purpose for them."*

*Romans 8:28 (NLT)*

Michelle grew up the sixth child out of seven. She found her groove as a mini-mom caretaker; her favorite dream was to someday be a wife and mommy. After graduating and getting married, Michelle and her husband tried for two years to conceive a child and were finally blessed with the perfect child.

Kimberly was precocious and full of laughter and smiles. And although she was exhausted for many of those early months, Michelle couldn't have been happier. Her lifelong dream of being a wife and mommy had come true.

Kim was a tiny child, with small bones and a petite bearing. It was easy to see her shoulder blades when she wore sundresses or while she was changing clothes. But one day those bones seemed to have moved. The doctor said he was 98 percent certain that everything was okay but, just in case, recommended surgery to remove a small tumor near her shoulder blade. What the doctor found were spider-like strands of a cancerous tumor that had begun to wrap themselves around Kim's tiny spine. It was a rare prenatal cancer that had been growing her whole short life. Holding their child close, Michelle and her husband walked into the storm around Kim's 18-month birthday.

Chemo treatments commenced, and Michelle had to learn how to clean ports, change dressings, and dole out meds, and she did it with proficiency and grace. Then radiation treatments were added in, moving their little family a few hours away into the Ronald McDonald house for several months. Michelle set up outings for her little trouper and pushed her in a stroller all over the area to parks and zoos and malls. And as all of the blonde, wispy strands of Kim's hair fell away, Michelle sewed cute little bonnets to cover her adorable bald head.

## I can do all things through him who gives me strength.

Michelle was so proficient in assisting with Kim's needs at the hospital that doctors often mistook her for nursing staff, ordering her to do this and that. She was constantly beside her daughter, through every twist and turn. She created craft projects for them to make in a hospital bed, and together they made artwork of every kind. Kim was even photographed as a poster child for the Ronald McDonald House ad campaign—smiles all around.

And eventually Kim was able to leave the children's hospital, diagnosed as cancer-free.

Life continued on, with another baby (sweet Elizabeth, another dream come true), and then a move or two, a change here and a challenge there. And each time, Michelle figured out how to make lemonade out of life's lemons.

Then divorce changed everything in her somewhat perfect little world. And there wasn't a thing she could do about it. She packed up and moved home to her parents' house, with only half of her dream of being a wife and mother struggling to survive.

Fast-forward several years. Another love had come, and husband Jim and his sweet children, Jimmy and Julie, gave Michelle another opportunity to fulfill her dreams of being a wife and mom. There were a lot of hardships in life, but she rolled with the punches and tried to make the best of each situation.

And then, through a series of visits to the doctor near Kim's college hours away from Michelle, it was discovered that something was wrong with Kim's heart. At first they thought it was a faulty valve, but during surgery discovered that her whole heart muscle needed to be replaced. After another few small procedures and not nearly enough time, it was obvious that both her heart and lungs were failing. Only five hospitals in the U.S. were capable of doing a double transplant, and all five of them turned her down. She was just too fragile.

So Michelle and Kim created another home in a hospital room and made the best of what they had. Kim's tracheotomy prevented further out-loud discussion, but Michelle became an expert at reading lips and intuitive guessing. And then, per Kim's request, Michelle set up a mini-ICU in their small-town home so Kim could go home for a few days. Heroically, Michelle made the difficult transfer from having around-the-clock nursing at their disposal to doing it all on her own, uncomplaining of the hardship.

They pulled it off. And then, as her body started shutting down, they journeyed back to the hospital one last time. Ever the fighter, Kim astounded the doctors with her stamina. But her damaged heart was working as hard as pedaling a 10-speed bike on first speed, and it couldn't—and didn't—last.

As Michelle prepared to lay her firstborn to rest, she curled Kim's hair, applied makeup, and painted her nails one last time. And she thanked God that Kim had re-established her relationship with Jesus and would suffer no more throughout eternity. That's where her hope had always come from and where it would stay. Philippians 4:13 was Kim's favorite verse: "I can do all things through him who gives me strength" (NIV).

She could face another day because she knew that God was with her. He had always helped her sort through the lemons well. Every time they came she had a choice to make, and once again, she chose well.

Now a pastor, Michelle has learned how to use the difficulties in her life to help people every single day. God has truly used her lemonade-making skills for his glory.

# REFLECT AND RESPOND

Have you encountered life's lemons, too?

_____

_____

_____

_____

How can you make the best outcome of your difficult situation?
God is with you, just like he was with Michelle and Kim.

_____

_____

_____

_____

I love how God can take our twists and turns in life to make beautiful connections happen in his timing.

# UNEXPECTED FRIENDSHIPS

## Lindsay May

*"After David had finished talking with Saul, he met Jonathan, the king's son. There was an immediate bond between them, for Jonathan loved David."*

1 Samuel 18:1 (NLT)

Part of human nature is to crave connection and relationships. Most often, we try to fulfill this need by surrounding ourselves with the people like us. The majority of our friendships are probably people who are in the same life stage and about the same age. They probably make a similar amount of money and dress alike. These are the people we seem to instantly gravitate toward out of familiarity and comfort.

As I was reading about young David in the Bible, his relationship with King Saul's son Jonathan struck me. I've always pictured David and Jonathan as two teenage guys running around together as best bros. But really, Jonathan could have been more like a father figure to David. If you do a little historical math, one could estimate that Jonathan was at least 10 to 15 years older than David, perhaps more. We know from the Bible that their friendship ran deep despite the fact they were an unlikely pair. One was a shepherd boy not old enough to go into battle, the other a skilled warrior prince. They should have been rivals competing for the king's throne, and they were probably in different life stages. Yet they had an immediate bond when they met, and encouraged and supported one another—spurring each other to fulfill God's plan and remaining friends to the end.

Such a friendship came into my life recently, seemingly out of nowhere. About one year ago, a woman I was acquainted with from church reached out to me through a Facebook message, admiring some photography work I had done recently. We chatted a while over messages and decided to meet up for coffee one evening. As we got to chatting, we realized how many connections and interests we shared. She was one of those people I felt like I could open up to and talk about anything, even though we had just met.

I am still amazed that in less than a year's time, this lady has become one of my closest friends, even though she has 20 more years of life experience than I do. I have been able to learn so much from simply watching the way she lives her life, fully committed to the Lord and her family. We have had incredibly different experiences in our lives, yet here we are together in the present. Our hearts have many of the same passions for the Church and to bring about God's best for our world. I love how God can take our twists and turns in life to make beautiful connections happen in his timing. God has known the end from the beginning, and he has had a purpose for all of our relationships—what he has planned, he will do (Isaiah 46:10-11).

In fact, one of the things I love the most about our friendship is our age difference. Her experiences and trials in life have shown me how to get through my own. 1 Thessalonians 5:11 says, "Therefore encourage one another and build each other up, just as in fact you are doing" (NIV). She has been there to pray for me over the phone when I've struggled with fear and anxiety. I can imagine that David and Jonathan influenced one another in a similar way. I'm sure that David never dreamed of becoming so close to the king's son—it was probably beyond his comprehension when he was tending sheep. But God wove their lives together to strengthen one another when they needed it the most and to bring about his purpose.

Ephesians 3:20-21 (NIV) says, "Now all glory to God, who is able, through his mighty power at work within us, to accomplish infinitely more than we might ask or think. Glory to him in the church and in Christ Jesus through all generations forever and ever!" I love that this verse says "through *all* generations." I never expected this friendship of mine to blossom the way it has. But it has taught me that we need to build relationships with those who are older and younger than us. There is so much beauty in diversity in our lives and the way we can help lift one another up through our experiences and perspectives.

When we ask God to bring deeper friendships in our lives, we may be surprised at who God decides to pair with us. Sometimes God will place someone in your life with whom you will have an instant and deep connection that may seemingly come out of nowhere, but God has a plan and a purpose. We just need to have willing and open hearts to be sensitive to where and *who* God might be leading us to.

# REFLECT AND RESPOND

Is there anyone you've been looking up to from afar? How might you reach out to them to get to know them better?

_____

_____

_____

_____

How diverse is your own group of friends? Do you need to branch out to gain a different perspective?

_____

_____

_____

_____

# ADOPTION WASN'T OUR IDEA

## Ginger Bailey

*"He predestined us for adoption to sonship through Jesus Christ, in accordance with his pleasure and will, to the praise of his glorious grace, which he has freely given us in the one he loves."*

*Ephesians 1:5-6 (NIV)*

Adoption has impacted our lives in a profound way and, whether you know it yet or not, it has impacted yours as well. You see, adoption isn't new, and it wasn't our idea. It was God's design, and it's interwoven throughout history and our lives.

During our sixth year of marriage, through the pain of infertility, God led us to adoption. It was one of the most beautiful and difficult seasons of our lives. We had anticipated a very long process, yet God had a very different timeline. From start to finish, our adoption took just seven months. This means our child had been conceived before our first application was even sent in! That, my sisters, is God's hand in orchestrating a life.

We adopted our oldest daughter when she was just a baby. In fact, we had the privilege of picking her up from the hospital. That experience completely changed our hearts in an instant. As we gazed upon her in that hospital room, the realization that she was now our child sank in, and the tears began to fall. We fell in love with this tiny baby, even when she couldn't give us much in return. We were captivated by her.

Did you know that's how God sees you? When God sent his son to earth, his plan for you was adoption, to make you his own child. Throughout scripture, God is clear on how he feels about adoption...about *you*!

Moses was adopted by Pharaoh's daughter, and his adoption was part of God's overall plan for the deliverance of Israel from Egypt (Exodus 2:1-10). When Esther's parents died, Mordecai, her cousin, took her as his own daughter (Esther 2:15). This adoption also led to a wonderful deliverance of the people of God.

In fact, Jesus himself was an adoptee. Joseph, who raised Jesus as his own, was not his biological father. Joseph gladly accepted Jesus, providing Him with all the love, encouragement, and guidance that a son needs from a father (Luke 1-2). His birth and adoption led to the deliverance of the *world*!

Throughout scripture, God is clear on how he feels about adoption...about you!

The Bible tells us that there is only one way for us to enter the kingdom of God—we must become God's *adopted* children through Jesus Christ. Ephesians 1:5-6 says, "He predestined us for adoption to sonship through Jesus Christ, in accordance with his pleasure and will, to the praise of his glorious grace, which he has freely given us in the one he loves" (NIV).

In adopting us through Christ, God shows the depth of his love. What a delightful model this presents to those who want to adopt a child. I found it interesting in researching adoption that under ancient Roman law, an adopted child became a new person. He received a new name, a new identity. Adoptees were legally separated from everything that made up their past and were given legal rights to all the wealth and fortunes of their new families! This is what we are able to give our daughter: a legal right to our fortune. A fortune of love, trust, honesty, reliability, stability, love for Jesus, a safe home, and a true, blue, gloriously imperfect (yet driven by love) family!

*Throughout scripture, God is clear on how he feels about adoption - about you!*

Because of adoption, our daughter has a new name, a new status, a new position. Our love, poured into her, created a bond of love that has grown and will continue to grow. She has a completely new life from that which she was born to. And God's love does the same for us.

# REFLECT AND RESPOND

Through adoption in Christ, you have a completely new life from that which you were born to (sin).

So let me ask you: What is your new name (identity)?

_____

_____

_____

_____

What is your new position in him? What life is he calling you to live now that you are his beloved, chosen, and adopted daughter?

_____

_____

_____

_____

# MAMA CLOIE NOLES

## Kandy Stevens

*"Then they cried out to the Lord in their trouble, and he brought them out of their distress."*

*Psalm 107:28 (NIV)*

I can't remember a world without her. She's my favorite confidante, sometimes my partner in hijinks, and she also happens to be my grandmother. I had the opportunity to live with her and my Papa during my graduate school days. We still giggle about some of our adventures, especially ones that drove my grandfather to fits of exasperation.

Second only to playing outside, sitting around the table listening to the tales of my family was one of my favorite activities as a child. My children often ask me to tell stories of growing up, a curiosity that was passed to them through the generations. I would always ask my grandparents, parents, aunts and uncles to tell me the stories of their lives. Imagining them in the younger years was always a fanciful time.

My Mama Cloie Noles was born at home to a farming family in the eastern Alabama foothills. She was the third of fifteen children, twelve of whom lived past infancy. Two constants punctuated her early years—working in the fields and going to church. With such a large immediate family and all their extended family within a few miles, there was never any real reason to leave home. "Going to town" just never crossed their minds. Her world was pretty small.

"We were poor, but we didn't know it," she has often told me. Though they lived in such isolation, it was, in her mind, a blessed and cherished existence. Everyone they saw lived the same lifestyle, so comparing just wasn't a part of their worldview.

## Prayer became a way of life and not just something to do on Sunday.

During a recent phone conversation, Mama, who is now 91, shared a story I had never heard before. My heart did little pitter-patters as she told of an event that forever changed her life. She was 16 years old, and it was a chilly Sunday morning. As she told me the story, it was clear she was watching the memory unfold in her imagination. "I had never seen my Daddy cry," she recalled. My curiosity was piqued, because I never knew my Great-Granddaddy Cunningham to be anything but happy and could not imagine him crying.

They'd had the radio on while getting ready for worship. It was to be only Sunday School that week, because the itinerant preacher came only every third Sunday. "My daddy was stuck on that," she said. "If you lived in his house, you were going to church."

Preparations for that Sunday were no different until the radio announced news that completely changed Mama's life. The previous quiet of that Sunday was punctuated by the grave news shared by the broadcaster. The date was December 7, 1941. My Granddaddy Cunningham began to bawl as details of the bombing of Pearl Harbor were relayed over the airwaves.

Alive during World War I, my great-grandfather knew this heinous atrocity would cause America to join a war that until that moment had been successfully avoided. "I think my Daddy cried because he knew my brother was old enough to go to war." And he did go, along with two of Mama's uncles. "Suddenly the world was a much bigger place."

Until this conversation, I never realized how my grandparents would remember the Pearl Harbor attack. One moment in the sheltered life of a sweet sixteen-year-old girl changed everything. The world became a larger and more turbulent place, but it was still one where spending time on your knees could change everything. As her world grew bigger, so too did her dependence on God. Prayer became a way of life and not just something to do on Sunday. And although one spent time in a POW camp, her uncles and brother did come home, and they appreciated all of her prayers.

# REFLECT AND RESPOND

For whom is God calling you to pray today?

_____

_____

_____

_____

# I KNOW—AND I THRIVE

## Mara Sorenson

*"For we live by believing and not by seeing."*

*2 Corinthians 5:7 (NLT)*

Four thousand, four hundred and twelve. That's how many days I prayed I would never hear the words the doctor was telling me. Six. That was the number of words it took to change everything. As I sat in the optometrist's office, my stomach hit the floor as he looked from my then 12-year-old son to me and said, "There's no doubt it's retinitis pigmentosa." The genetic disorder that would cause this son of mine to go blind was now a reality. Life altered, faith challenged, enormous questions asked.

While I have had thousand of conversations with God, all of a sudden the conversations changed. "Please," "why," "how," and "help" became the words spoken most often when talking with God. While I believe that God can and does heal, I also know that he sometimes chooses to use the hardships of life for his greater purpose. And it's in that truth that we now live this life.

Day after day I claim God's promises out loud. These are my "I know" moments. I know God gives good gifts to his children. I know that he will never leave us nor forsake us. I know that he is faithful to complete the work he began in my son. I know he holds all of his tomorrows. I know that God prepares good works in advance for his followers, and my son is proudly a follower of Christ. I know that God sees every tear shed from our eyes and someday he will wipe them from our faces. I know that even if my son doesn't see beauty on earth that he will see beauty beyond words, with perfect vision, someday in heaven.

> ## We walk by faith, not by sight.

To survive, let alone thrive, I have to get my eyes off of the situation and on to the cross. And this is my daily challenge. The reality of a white cane in our entryway leaning against my son's shoes is a harsh reality. The Braille papers scattered around the house feels like a slap in the face every time I see them. The falls, the bumps and bruises, the explanations—all these daily things can sap the joy and faith right from our hearts. And yet, God is good. That I *know*!

Our family has adopted a motto verse that hangs in our dining room. 2 Corinthians 5:7 says, "We walk by faith, not by sight" (ESV). I look at that verse every day and give thanks. While that verse speaks to our spiritual life, it also speaks to the physical life that we now walk alongside our son.

God has not just given us life, but life abundant. This is the life in which we not just survive, but thrive. To thrive when life is full of thornless roses is easy. To thrive when life is nothing but thorns, takes God. It takes a spiritual act of our will to see the anchor of faith in the storm of life. To stand upon the goodness of God and the faithfulness of his promises sometimes feels like the hardest thing to do, and yet we do it. We choose to thrive because just surviving is not what we are called to do. And above all, I know that these momentary troubles will pale in comparison to the splendor that awaits us all in heaven.

# REFLECT AND RESPOND

When life gets difficult we can tend to shut down and isolate ourselves. What circumstances have "blindsided" you in your life?

_____

_____

_____

_____

Who can you turn to when you feel this way?

_____

_____

_____

_____

# THE REARVIEW MIRROR

## Julie Fisk

*"But blessed is the man who trusts me, GOD,*
*the woman who sticks with GOD.*
*They're like trees replanted in Eden,*
*putting down roots near the rivers—*
*Never a worry through the hottest of summers,*
*never dropping a leaf,*
*Serene and calm through droughts,*
*bearing fresh fruit every season."*

Jeremiah 17:7-8 (MSG)

My younger self adjusted my seat belt and fiddled with the cruise control as I settled in for the three-hour drive home. With my bridesmaid duties complete and the wedding reception winding down, I let my mind wander down memory lane as my car ate up miles of pavement through the prairies of western Minnesota. Fond memories of college hijinks with the bride and groom slowly turned to thoughts of the cute groomsman "randomly" assigned to be my escort down the aisle and my friends' attempts to set us up.

I silently berated myself for being, once again, too shy to vie for his attention amongst all the other single ladies. Berating shifted to planning, and I began plotting how I could finagle a second contact with him since we both lived in the Twin Cities. I was tired of being shy around guys and convinced myself that it was time to do something about it.

My mind made up, I paused as a thought passed through my mind: *Perhaps you ought to pray about that decision.*

Thinking it was a good idea, my simple flippant prayer went up. "Dear Jesus, should I contact that groomsman?" With my prayer complete, my thoughts turned to graduate school obligations and the miles of road still looming as I reached down and flipped on the radio.

A popular country song immediately filled the car with lyrics about driving away from a guy, without a backward glance in the rearview mirror, with no plans to ever contact him again.

I paused, my glance flicking to the rearview mirror and the wedding reception I was rapidly leaving behind. I snapped off the radio and prayed again, this time with focus: "Lord, I have no idea if you spoke to me through that song or not, but I'm not going to contact him. I'm going to trust you."

What I didn't know, couldn't know, was that a funny, handsome, extroverted, sweet guy was, only two weeks in the future, going to ask me to go for a walk. And because I wouldn't be involved with anyone else, that shy version of my younger self was going to say yes.

But God knew. And God knew that I would have turned down that walk if I had set up a date with the groomsman.

Saying yes to that walk turned into saying "I do" to my best friend, to the father of my children, to the man with whom I've built a loving home and a life, a man who knows me at my worst and loves me anyway. I am married to the man who is the perfect fit for me.

# Perhaps you ought to pray about that decision.

Had I not listened to the still, small voice on that lonely drive home, would I have ended up marrying my husband of almost 15 years? I don't know. I do know that, had I not listened to that quiet voice, at best, I would have met my husband only after unnecessary complication and, most certainly, after serious heartache.

That night, in the middle of a lonely stretch of highway, I had no clue what God had planned when I was asked to trust and wait. God's plans for me were so much bigger and better than the plans that I had for myself.

# REFLECT AND RESPOND

Is there a situation in which God is asking you to trust and wait for him?

_____

_____

_____

_____

What decisions, big or small, is God asking you to hand to him in prayer? What is your response?

_____

_____

_____

_____

# OH, TO DELIGHT IN YOU, LORD

## Kate Washleski

*"The Lord your God is in your midst, a mighty one who will save. He will rejoice over you with gladness. He will quiet you by His love. He will exult over you with loud singing."*

*Zephaniah 3:17 (ESV)*

The "recovering perfectionist" in me has a hard time understanding and experiencing what the Bible describes as God's delight in me. Me, who forgets to pack an extra pair of clothes for my son at daycare. Me, who loses her temper over something small with my husband. Me, who feels like I just don't have what it takes sometimes. Yes, the Bible says he delights in you and me.

God recently met me in an everyday moment with my newborn daughter to help me understand his delight in me. I was holding her, watching her breathe in and out, sleeping so peacefully in my arms. The whole house was empty, except for the two of us. She wasn't performing for me, cooing or smiling or wiggling her cute little legs. She wasn't doing anything other than sleeping. There wasn't anything she could do to make me love her any more or less. I looked at her and thought, *You're perfect.*

And all of a sudden I realized, through the Holy Spirit's teaching, that this is what it means to delight. I had heard of delighting in the Lord and that he delights in us, but until that moment it hadn't been real for me. As I delighted in holding my baby girl, I began to worship, right there in the rocking chair. How sweet of God to teach me more of his love for me through my love for her.

God used that moment to help me get a glimpse of his delight in us and his grace towards us. We don't have to be cooking or cleaning or checking things off our lists. We truly bring him such joy, even when we aren't "doing" anything.

Psalm 147:11 says, "The Lord delights in those who fear him, who put their hope in his unfailing love" (NIV). When we breathe in and out and let the Lord hold us in the midst of whatever we're facing, he takes great delight. When we bring our triumphs and our shortcomings to him, knowing that he loves us always, and when he corrects us in the way that only he can, it's because he delights in us.

Even though we don't have to be doing anything "special" to earn God's delight, we have an opportunity to consider the things in our lives that bring us delight and to ask God what he might want to teach us through it. I know my time with my kids has become sweeter since that morning worship in the rocking chair. When I find myself delighting in my husband, kids, friends, watching things that I've planted grow, and other things in my everyday life, they have begun to serve as reminders of God's delight in me. And the freedom to stop trying so hard and just let God hold me enables me to find even more delight in whatever today holds.

# REFLECT AND RESPOND

What's one thing or person in your life that you delight in?

_____

_____

_____

_____

How do you feel as you consider how much more God delights in you?

_____

_____

_____

_____

Might God be trying to speak to you through that person or thing, to whisper his love to your heart?

_____

_____

_____

_____

## He will rejoice over you with gladness.

# UNDER CAIRN-STRUCTION

## Terrin Boozikee

*"The rain came down, the streams rose, and the winds blew and beat against that house; yet it did not fall, because it had its foundation on the rock."*

*Matthew 7:25 (NIV)*

Rocks have always fascinated me; as a young child, I used to collect them. Recently, my love of rocks took on a new form when a dear friend of mine introduced me to cairns. A cairn is a heap of stones set up as a landmark or monument.

Recently, I spent a beautiful Minnesota weekend at the lake. While awaiting my turn for a ride on the speedboat, I decided to spend some time combing the beach and collecting rocks. Breeze blowing through my wavy hair, I picked up flat rocks, conglomerate rocks, and red rocks. Some I picked up only to throw back later. Others I didn't realize I wanted until I began to construct my cairn.

Building a cairn feels like a puzzle. You need a solid base so the rest of your rocks will not topple when wind and rain threaten the cairn's strength. Next, you must layer the rocks in such a way that they hold each other up. You want to twist, turn, flip, and adjust your rocks so you can find a secure spot for each to sit. Eventually each rock finds its place in the cairn, and you are left in awe of the simplicity of the rocks' beauty.

I have found life to be like a big cairn. I've tried to piece together stones with a foundation of pride, and when rains fall, they come crashing down as soon as I realize just how human I am. I have tried to find security in the arms of others, in financial well-being, and even in my spotless reputation. At one time or another, those cairns have fallen. The arms of another are not enough to outlast the doubts and depression. A good financial standing isn't all that helpful when there are problems that transcend monetary value. And my spotless reputation as a perfect teacher's kid doesn't do much for me in the real world. I've come to find that the only life cairn that stands is one that includes the security I find in Jesus Christ.

Cairns remind me of Psalm 40:2, which says, "He lifted me out of the slimy pit, out of the mud and mire; he set my feet on a rock and gave me a firm place to stand" (NIV).

God lifted me out of my pit, and I can trust in the security that he provides.

Back on the beach, waves washing over my feet, I continued to build my cairn. Some of the rocks I used were still covered with dirt and sand, but as they found their place on their solid foundation, I knew they wouldn't be moved when the winds and rain came upon them later that afternoon.

Cairns teach me that we all have a place. There are some oddly shaped rocks, but those can be great pieces for the top! There are flat rocks for stacking, and there are chunky rocks for solidity. On your own, you may feel like a rock that is only good to be thrown back into the deep waters of the lake, but God sees a beautiful purpose within you. An important distinction that took me many years to learn is that God doesn't love us for what we can do for him. In fact, there is nothing we can offer him really. He loves us so much just as we are, and he will use us just as we are.

As I finished my cairn that afternoon on the beach, I was reminded that there is a place for me in God's story. Cairns show me that God makes beautiful things out of misfit things, because he is our great redeemer. God uses our broken lives to showcase his deep, fervent love for his children. He showers us with grace, and our stories can be a testament to that. Cairns instill in me a confidence that my strong foundation is found in Christ alone.

*He loves us so much just as we are, and he will use us just as we are.*

# REFLECT AND RESPOND

How might the stones of your life fit into the cairn God wants to construct for you?

_____

_____

_____

_____

Do you believe that God can redeem every story—even yours?

_____

_____

_____

_____

# CHOOSING TO FLOURISH

## *Anonymous*

*"When I open up in song to you,*
*I let out lungsful of praise,*
*my rescued life a song.*
*All day long I'm chanting*
*about you and your righteous ways,*
*While those who tried to do me in*
*slink off looking ashamed."*

*Psalm 71:23-24 (MSG)*

Twelve years ago, my husband of 16 years, my missionary partner and the father of my children, walked away like a stranger. I was left with four precious children in a land far away, feeling betrayed, emotionally raw, and physically numb. My world as it had been fell away. It was just me, my four kids, and God (and his people, but that is another story). Amidst the chaos of preparing to return to the U.S., the Lord asked me in a still voice: "Will you be bitter or will you trust and allow me to flourish your lives in the pain?" My simple daily prayer became, "Lord, may we not be people of bitterness but flourish in the midst of this pain."

As the plane touched down in U.S. soil in a city I barely knew, we started life again. My to-do list looked like this: Unpack our three bags, find a laundromat to wash clothes, eat peanut butter sandwiches at 3:00 a.m. as we all worked to get over jet lag, get a driver's license, put meals on the table, register my two oldest kids for school, start my daughter on TB medication after finding out she had contracted it overseas, lease a temporary car, learn to pump gas using a debit card, start working, and more. The daily fleshing out of life blurred on overwhelmingly, but in the midst of it all, a small voice said, "I am here. Will you praise me?"

*Lord, sing and praise you? I don't feel like singing.*

But the Lord said, "Sing."

So I sang, and as I sang the tears flowed. As I praised, the cares lifted. As I prayed, by his grace, God did his work. He provided our daily bread—literally—in the form of a precious elderly man who baked delicious fresh bread for us. He sent his people to take my kids to the playground, keeping them awake to overcome their jet lag. He provided a means for me to work and friends for my children. He gave words to touch the hard places and heal the unexplainable pain.

Each night, as the kids and I would gather, I would read to them and pray. We also discussed what we were thankful for. Psalms 107:1, "Give thanks to the Lord for he is good; his love endures forever," (NIV) kept running through my mind. So we gave thanks. Thanks for the squirrels who entertained us as we looked out our dining room window. Thanks for the suitcases that did make it on the plane. Thanks for family, as well as for new and old friends, who gave of their time and funds to help us in those early days.

And we thanked God for his grace that made it possible to avoid the temptation to shut down in the face of abandonment and betrayal, to not lash out in the midst of emotional pain and loss, but to speak honestly. He was and is faithful in the midst of it all.

The days have since turned into years. Years of working through pain, joyfully watching my children grow and mature, working through the tough stuff and sometimes getting "stuck" but always by his grace becoming "unstuck" and flourishing again.

Most of us have experienced trauma or loss in our lives. In the moment of shock, trauma, questioning, and anger, our human-ness says, "I was sinned against. It's not fair, and I have a right to be angry, sad, disillusioned, bitter."

Yes, we feel those feelings. But God calls and enables us by his Holy Spirit to choose to flourish through prayer, praise, and thankfulness. What we *do* with our circumstance is what will either allow us to turn trauma into a deeper joy and spiritual depth or become bitter and robbed of the amazing life God has planned for us.

# But the Lord said, "Sing."

One day recently, my middle son got in the car for our morning commute. Unlike most mornings, with four of us packed in with backpacks, sports equipment, and computer cases, it was just the two of us.

He said, "Yesterday the teacher asked our class what we would change in our lives if we could."

I asked him what his answer had been.

"I would change nothing," he replied.

"Really? Not your dad leaving?"

"Nope, nothing. I wouldn't be who I am if those events would not have happened. I am glad to be where God has me and who I am."

I cried as I saw the fruit of my prayers and God's faithfulness. In what had been a very messy and painful life (and sometimes still is), God by his severe grace has allowed us to flourish and not be hindered by bitterness. Thank you, Lord!

Sisters, by his grace, choose to flourish! He is faithful.

# REFLECT AND RESPOND

Have you experienced pain in your life that has caused bitterness to take root?

_____

_____

_____

_____

What steps can you take today to flourish despite your difficult circumstances?

_____

_____

_____

_____

Looking back,
I realized that I had
never fully grasped
that every one
of my words spoke
either life or death.

# WORDS OF LIFE

## Kelli Patrick

*"The tongue has the power of life and death."*

*Proverbs 18:21 (NIV)*

About a year ago, I had one of the largest wake-up calls in my life. As I sat on the phone with my 19-year-old niece, she shared how she was feeling our friendship had hit a rocky spot. She felt that my jokes and words were tearing her apart. Immediately my heart sank and tears fell down my face. We had always had a great relationship, and I had always assumed that she knew my feelings toward her. Our normal conversations were filled with jokes and humor, but nothing offensive or discouraging, at least in my mind.

I was completely blindsided. I had never meant to be a bully or a source of pain, but at that moment our relationship had hit rock bottom. I spent many nights thinking to myself how all our conversations were built around lighthearted humor, and as a youth pastor I wondered if this was a theme in my relationships.

A large part of my job and calling was built around speaking life into people, and a feeling of failure filled my heart.

At that moment, Proverbs 18:21, a verse that I had heard since I was young, hit me hard: "The tongue has the power of life and death, and those who love it will eat its fruit" (NIV).

I wondered, *When is the last time I told my niece how proud of her I am?* I had always assumed she knew. I would have considered myself to be an encourager, but as I started to examine other relationships in my life I wondered: *Even though I feel like an encourager, are the words verbally coming out of my mouth? Am I looking for opportunities to lift people up? Have I become the kind of person that even I don't want to be around?*

I knew I was feeling loved in the relationship with my niece. However, was I only on the receiving end and not taking the opportunities to share my love and appreciation of the woman God was forming her into?

Looking back, I realized I had never fully grasped that every one of my words spoke either life or death. Every single word.

From talking to the cashier at the grocery store to laughing with my niece on the phone, I have the chance to bring someone death or life. As I pass someone in a store aisle, do I look away or take a moment to bring some joy with a simple smile? Critiquing my interactions, I realized that I was failing severely. Looking back on time spent with my family, the people I love the most, I realized I was missing my opportunity to encourage.

As I look through the New Testament, I am continually reminded that Jesus took time to encourage each person he interacted with. Whether it was one of his disciples, the people he spent every day with, or someone he met for only moments, he took time to encourage and speak life into every person he came in contact with. Every morning I wake up with the knowledge that words as simple as "hello" and as meaningful as "I am proud of you" speak life or death.

# REFLECT AND RESPOND

Today, will you realize the power of every word that comes from your mouth?

_____

_____

_____

_____

Will you purposefully challenge yourself to speak life in every conversation?

_____

_____

_____

_____

# MY HEALTH AWAKENING

## Ashley Darkenwald

*"For God has not given us a spirit of fear and timidity, but of power, love, and self-discipline."*

*2 Timothy 1:7 (NLT)*

My life changed radically, albeit gradually, the day I realized God cared more about my health than I did. An excerpt from my book, *Living Wellness*, sums up my journey:

*I used to get sick a lot. Even as a fitness professional, my colleagues would say, "You are the healthiest sick person I know." I blamed my constant illness on bad genes and having children that brought home the bug. Sinus infections, common colds, pink-eye (yes, as an adult), strep throat, influenza, and the stomach flu. I had it all, all the time. However, there was a gradual awareness that my illnesses were wearing on my family and me. I hit the breaking point of being sick and tired over three years ago, and I have not looked back.*

In addition to being sick all of the time, I also used to struggle with my weight:

*In high school, I decided to change course from a three-season athlete to a theater performer. This dramatically reduced my activity level, and I gained weight. If you had asked my friends, they would not have classified me as overweight, but you could imagine the surprise when I lost 20 pounds in college from a consistent running routine! I did not start out running miles and miles per day. I made a commitment to get to the gym every day for at least three minutes. Yes, just three minutes. I heard a motivational speaker say that anyone can make time for three minutes per day for something important. Three minutes per day of exercise for one semester: This simple commitment developed into a lifelong journey of health and whole-person wellness.*

Like my long-ago decision to commit to at least three minutes a day for better health, God deserves a commitment as well. God deserves 100 percent of my commitment to him, in all areas of my life: not 70 percent, not 80 percent, not even 95 percent. God deserves my best, and my best means being as healthy as I can be physically, nutritionally, and spiritually.

My journey toward God-honoring health took grit, endurance, and determination. Nobody looked out for my health, what I put in my mouth, or if I moved my legs and arms on a regular basis, except for me.

My transformation took place over years, not overnight. We serve a loving, patient, and gentle God who, if we allow, will lead us on a path toward better health, bring key people into our lives who can support us, and give us the strength to make good decisions when it comes to food, movement, and the temptations to be lazy or lack self-discipline.

Today I have energy to serve Christ in new ways, including a recent missions trip to Africa and a new business I started, because of how I nourish my body and honor God with my daily health and wellness choices. I deny the lies of shame that come from comparing my body image to anyone else's. Instead, I believe the truth that I am an image bearer of God (Genesis 1:27), that God has a good purpose for my life (John 15:16), and that he is not finished with me yet (Philippians 1:6)!

If God is speaking to you about your health right now, or if you feel a tug on your heart to honor him with your physical health, ask God to show you how much he loves you and your health and well-being. Ask him to show you the continued purpose for your life. And then, listen. Have faith. Have courage. He will meet you right where you are.

*He will meet you right where you are.*

# REFLECT AND RESPOND

Have you invited God into your health journey recently?

_____

_____

_____

_____

What is God saying to you?

_____

_____

_____

_____

As you listen, be prepared to respond. Your path toward healthier living will be full of small hills and giant mountains. But every step will bring you closer to who you were created to be if you daily invite God into your journey.

# CHOOSING GRATITUDE OVER GRIEF

## Kristin Demery

*"Be cheerful no matter what; pray all the time; thank God no matter what happens. This is the way God wants you who belong to Christ Jesus to live."*

*1 Thessalonians 5:16-18 (MSG)*

I felt immobilized by grief last week. Maybe it was the relentless rain, the gloomy gray clouds an external gauge for my internal turmoil. My girls were restless, and so was I. It could have been self-pity; a series of days where even the thought of my to-do list feels paralyzing. I'm in the midst of a busy month, and I've found myself wishing that I was better at saying no. Maybe it's the fact that I've heard one too many stories of hurt and heartache lately, and I'm wearied by this world.

But really, all of these things merely added up to a vague discontent until a sweet text from my sister Kendra became the tipping point one day. She was passing on a story from a friend, something that reminded us all of the loss of our oldest sister Katrina.

"Wow—I miss her!" my mom texted back.

"Me too," Kendra replied.

"Me three," I responded.

Even though it's been several years since she died from breast cancer, every once in a while the grief rises up unexpectedly. This morning, though the text was sweet and my memory sweeter, I absorbed it like a physical blow. As my children tugged on my knees to gain my attention, chubby fingers smeared with peanut butter from breakfast reaching up to grasp mine, I felt the weight settle on me. Smiling through tears, I grabbed the excuse of getting out the *My Little Pony* coloring books to wipe my eyes.

And I wondered: *What do you do when you try to reach for gratitude and find yourself grasping only air?* Though I am surrounded by daily graces, that day I felt only the burdens and none of the blessings.

*Only where there has been great loss can God show us his great gain.*

We hear it said that love is a choice. It's true: There are times when my husband and I are at odds, and I make an intentional choice to love. To forgive. To accept him, just as he is. And he extends the same grace to me.

Aren't we also called to be intentionally grateful as much as we are called to intentionally love? To make an intentional choice to recognize the blessings in our lives?

Today, I'm grateful because I choose to be grateful:

*For grace and the salvation of the cross.*

*For the necessities of life I have in abundance.*

*For the loving husband and daughters who encourage me to follow my dreams.*

*For family and friends that walk through this life beside me.*

*For good health.*

*For good books!*

*For freedom.*

*For the ability to help others.*

*For things that aren't necessary but I love them anyway: pretty dishtowels, chunky coffee mugs, chocolate, and anything from Anthropologie.*

And, today, I'll add a new one: For the sweet memories I have of my sister Katrina. My life is better for having had her as my sister.

A friend of mine once wrote: "Only where there has been great loss can God show us his great gain." And it's true. Even though the tough days or seasons may hurt the most, it's the painful things, the rainy days, the waves of grief that have taught me joy.

# REFLECT AND RESPOND

What daily graces can you thank God for, even during days and seasons of hardship?

_____

_____

_____

_____

# I GOT MY WIFE BACK

## Dawn Zimmerman

*"Love one another as I have loved you."*

*John 15:12 (ESV)*

J ust days after receiving a state honor for my work, I put in my notice. Since I was a child, I remember wanting to be a journalist so I could tell other people's stories. By age 25, I had been promoted to editor for a Gannett newspaper. It came with long hours and a brain constantly wired to work. And I knew it would need to change before we started a family.

A couple months after leaving to start my own business, my husband and I reconnected with a small group from our church and started the evening going around in a circle sharing the best part about our summer. My husband was next.

A man of few words, he said, "I got my wife back."

I could feel my heart sink to my stomach and a lump develop in my throat. I was speechless; almost breathless. I never knew he lost her. In the months leading up to my resignation, he never once asked me to leave or gave me an idea that I was putting my career before him.

As the words came out of his mouth, the memories flooded my mind. All the missed dinners. All the times I said I was leaving in five minutes and arrived home an hour later.

We had each spent the first part of our lives thinking—even dreaming—about getting married someday. Here I was not even two years in, and I had missed the point. I was crushed. He deserved better. We deserved better.

I left that evening committing to never being lost again. I realized that I hadn't left what I thought was my dream career to be the mom I wanted to be. I left it to be the wife I wanted to be.

That conviction has grown over the years. Now, with two young kids, I have realized I want a marriage that makes other people want to get married. That's the legacy I want to give to my kids—and others in our world.

That takes commitment and some radical moves. I have had no greater teacher on this journey than Jesus.

When we got married ten years ago, we engraved John 15:12 inside our rings. It's not the typical marriage verse from Ephesians or the renowned love verses from 1 Corinthians 13. Yet in a few short, simple words, it provides a complete guide to not just a happy marriage, but one that would make others want to get married: "Love one another as I have loved you" (ESV).

That love is unconditional, as my husband has quietly shown me. It means loving when the person is being unlovable and showing respect even when the person doesn't deserve it. It means not getting lost in my own dreams because a dream we share will always be better than one I dreamt alone.

I don't desire a perfect marriage. That would miss the whole point. I want a real marriage that weathers the challenges of this life. I want one that's full of forgiveness because I will fall short, and I want my kids to learn the power of forgiveness, too. Accepting Jesus into my heart changed my life, and relationships are one of the best ways to reveal that.

*I have had no greater teacher on this journey than Jesus.*

Marriage is a covenant, not a contract. It's a commitment, not a compromise. My commitment is not to marriage. It's to my husband. Marriage may seem replaceable in this world. But my husband is irreplaceable.

I want our relationship with one another to reflect our relationship with God. That starts with loving one another as he loves us. It's a daily, lifelong commitment, and I look forward to loving the journey.

# REFLECT AND RESPOND

How can you love others as God loves you?

_____

_____

_____

_____

What do your actions within your relationships reveal about what you value?

_____

_____

_____

_____

# IT'S TIME TO FIGHT

## Jill Moltumyr

*"So we're not giving up. How could we! Even though on
the outside it often looks like things are falling apart on us,
on the inside, where God is making new life, not a day goes
by without his unfolding grace."*

2 Corinthians 4:17 (MSG)

I grew up thinking that if something was the will of God, it
would be easy to do. Somehow, God would open the doors that
you knew were the right doors because there was just a hint of
beautiful bright light coming from underneath the door. As you
cracked the door to begin this journey, a flood of glorious light
would envelop you.

Then you would know that the right door had been chosen and
you were on the right path. But I have learned that while God is
light that penetrates the darkness, his leading and guiding does
not always look like a bright light showing the path towards a safe
arrival.

In July, my family took off on an adventure of a lifetime. After a lot of waiting for God to speak, we had heard a very specific word from God that he wanted us to move to Tennessee to work with my husband's former youth pastors. It was a leap of faith bigger than any he had asked of us thus far. In fact, it felt a lot like free-falling through the air as we prepared to make the transition.

On the journey to our new home, there were very few bright light moments. Those two days were filled with delay after delay. Our newly loaded moving truck malfunctioned the entire way down to Tennessee. These truck delays led to more than six hours of extra drive time and most likely a few gray hairs. We also had hours of heavy rain and even sat in our vehicles parked on the highway due to construction.

I remember specifically a moment driving through the hills of Kentucky on day two where I simply felt I was done. We had been through so much, and I was simply ready to be at our new home. At that moment, our trailer tire literally blew up. It honestly was one of those moments where you get to see what you are made of. Yes, I cried a few tears and my hands were shaking as I phoned the rental company to send their repair truck. I also prayed a lot of prayers for safety as we sat on the side of that hill.

I continued to watch our yellow moving truck struggle the remainder of the trip as we headed into the mountains of Tennessee. At times, we were going 35 miles per hour up the hills. That slow speed was all our truck could handle.

Before leaving Minnesota, I remember feeling a nudge from God that this next season of life was going to be a bit different from the waiting season we were exiting.

And as I followed that slow moving truck, these words came to mind:

*Sometimes when you're trying to get to where God wants you to be, you have to fight for it. You're going to have to push, pull, and persevere, because sometimes he wants **you** to fight.*

During those fighting times, something happens inside us. Our backs are strengthened, and our focus is set. There is an objective, and we must move forward.

*It was a leap of faith bigger than any he had asked of us thus far.*

There are times this journey of life may seem to take an exceptional amount of fighting, but even then we can find peace. Paul's life as a perfect example of this: "I have learned how to be content with whatever I have. I know how to live on almost nothing or with everything. I have learned the secret of living in every situation, whether it is with a full stomach or empty, with plenty or little. For I can do everything through Christ, who gives me strength," (Philippians 4:11-13, NLT).

When we find ourselves fully relying on God, we discover the strength he gives us to fight and the peace that he will be with us through each difficult step of our journey.

I pray that you will remember the fight is worth it.

# REFLECT AND RESPOND

What is God asking you to fight for right now?

_____

_____

_____

_____

How can you find peace during this time?

_____

_____

_____

_____

# WHAT I DIDN'T KNOW I WAS MISSING

## Annie Egeland

*"You did not choose Me but I chose you, and appointed you that you would go and bear fruit, and that your fruit would remain."*

*John 15:16 (NASB)*

rowing up, my family attended church regularly, even religiously. Despite three years of confirmation classes, I never developed a true relationship with the Lord.

My husband's experience was similar, so by the time we finished college we had given up on going to church. Since my mother had passed away when I was 14 and my father died when I was 24, I was used to feeling independent and relying on myself.

To be honest, I felt no need for a spiritual component in my life.

That changed for us in the late 1970s, however. My husband began working with someone who shared the Gospel with him, and he began reading his Bible and got to know Jesus personally.

My husband is nothing if not persistent. If he wants something, he'll figure out a way to get it. One day, he came home with a new Bible that he had bought. As a young married couple, money was tight and $5 felt like a lot of money. I was mad that he'd spent the money but was more irritated that he wouldn't give up talking about things I just wasn't interested in.

"You spent five dollars on *that*?!" I asked him. I couldn't understand why it was so important to him.

He had been praying and talking to me for the better part of a year when we got invited to a Bible study and prayer group. Tired of his nagging, I finally gave in and told him, "Fine! One time and one time only, and then you can never ask me again!"

It was late November, and our second daughter was just two weeks old. When we arrived at the family's house, they invited us to share dinner with them. They couldn't have been nicer, and after dinner I found myself sitting with a large group of people, singing songs and sharing from the Bible.

It's hard to describe the experience completely—all I know was that as I sat and listened, I had the most overwhelming urge to stand up and run out of the house and down the long driveway. Thankfully a part of me realized that this would be ridiculous! Racing out of someone's house was completely out of character for me. As we left later that night, I realized there was a struggle going on in my mind and spirit and that I had a choice to make.

The next morning as I thought about the previous night and wrestled with my thoughts, I finally said: *Jesus, if you are real, I give up.* This small step toward God was the catalyst that started a whole new way of life with Jesus. I felt like I was a new person. I *knew* I was a new person.

Since that experience, I've discovered what I didn't even know I was missing. That's the mercy of God—his plans for our story are so much better than our own plans. I was perfectly content to be a wife and a mother and have the life we led. But God's grace broke through my complacency and reached out to me, even when I had no desire for him.

*I felt like I was a new person.*
*I knew I was a new person.*

# REFLECT AND RESPOND

How have God's plans intersected with your own and changed your story?

_____

_____

_____

_____

How might God want to use your story to reach those who are far from him?

_____

_____

_____

_____

# A LITTLE ENCOURAGEMENT

### Nancy Holte

*"Therefore encourage one another and build one another up, just as you are doing."*

*1 Thessalonians 5:11 (ESV)*

Sometimes the simplest of words can encourage a person, offer a measure of hope, or just let someone know that you are on their side. My friend, Pat, was a master of well-placed words. The minute I saw her handwriting on an envelope in my mailbox I knew I would be blessed by her message.

Two days after hosting a neighborhood tea, I got this sweet message: "Dear Nancy, here it is Saturday evening and I feel like I experienced a magical trip to London today at your house! What a delight to be your guest at a genuine high tea! Queen Elizabeth would have felt right at home. Thank you, Nancy. Fondly, Pat." At the bottom of the note was a little stamped red heart. The stamped heart was as much a part of her signature as her name.

I received many notes from Pat in our 37 years of being neighbors: congratulatory notes, notes of encouragement, ones to remind me of her prayers, or simple birthday greetings! It mattered not whether I sent her a card on her birthday–come mid-June there was always one in my box. To be honest, I don't even know how she found out the date of my birth, but she never missed it. Even three weeks before she died, she sent me an email with her usual encouraging birthday greetings.

I wasn't the only one to receive Pat's notes. She probably wrote thousands in her lifetime. At her funeral this summer, the question was posed: How many in the church had received a note from Pat at some point in time? Every hand went up! One might say it was Pat's mission in life to make people feel good. And she did it well.

Her daughter told me that Pat even made it a point to encourage hotel maids and wait staff when she was on business trips with her husband. She would get to know the maids who serviced her room and leave them little notes and a tip each day she was there. At the end of the week she'd leave the wait staff some monetary encouragement as well along with one of her notes. Though I'm sure the staff always appreciated the cash, my guess is that her words were the real gift. Pat had a way of making everyone she met feel valued and loved.

Another daughter told me a story about Pat's notes that epitomizes her generosity and caring spirit. In the last few weeks of her life, it was necessary to transport her by ambulance to a nearby hospital. Her daughter met her at the hospital as Pat awaited surgery. The first thing Pat said to her daughter was, "I'll have to write a note to the ambulance driver." Always giving!

Sending notes may not seem like the making of a successful life and isn't even close to all the things Pat actually did. In fact, when I read her obituary I thought to myself, "I'm going to have to up my game if I expect my obituary to read half this well." Pat gave of herself consistently, abundantly, and with great purpose. Whether she was sending you a note, greeting you at the grocery store, or having tea with you at her kitchen table, her words were always words of encouragement. She cared well for her family, her friends, and even for people she didn't know. I was blessed to be the recipient of her kindness.

In Pat's memory, I plan on sending a few encouraging note-cards of my own. It only takes a few minutes, and I know from personal experience it can make a world of difference.

*Therefore encourage one another and build one another up, just as you are doing.*

# REFLECT AND RESPOND

How about you? Who can you encourage today? There is power in your words!

_____

_____

_____

_____

# BEYOND A DOUBT

## Kristen Ostrem

*"With good will render service, as to the Lord, and not to men, knowing that whatever good thing each one does, this he will receive back from the Lord...."*

*Ephesians 6:7-8 (NASB)*

From as far back as I can remember, I knew I would end up in Africa," she told me. "But I didn't like the idea at all, because I don't like bugs and dirt, and I didn't even think about the snakes."

Marlys was honest with me from the beginning. The beautiful 86-year-old mother of three, grandmother of nine, great-grandmother of 26, and retired missionary to Africa recently became my friend and shared her story with me. The thought of Africa was always within Marlys, she said. She grew up in a missions-minded church in Minneapolis, was raised to follow God, and met her future husband at the age of 16. It was about the second or third date that Del stated, "Someday I am going to Africa, and if you're not willing to go along, I am not going to spend any more time or money on you!"

"Words to that effect," she said, chuckling. "Luckily I knew this was the best thing that had come along so far, so I told him that I, too, knew that I was going to end up in Africa. That sealed my fate."

Three years later at the age of 19, Marlys became Del's bride. She and Del had three children and pastored in Minnesota for seven years before moving to Tanzania.

Their 30-year career in Africa involved Bible School work and village evangelism in Tanzania, as well as village evangelism and publishing literature in Malawi. Del was then asked to move to Kenya, where he was appointed Area Director for all of East Africa and started the East Africa School of Theology.

# What's more important than loving God and doing his will?

"I went with an inferiority complex, because I was neither a preacher nor a teacher, and I had three small children," Marlys said. "A few weeks after we arrived [in Tanzania], I heard another missionary say, 'I can't wait until my kids go back to boarding school so I can get back to missions work.' Here I was with three small children, and I thought, 'My missions work will start at home.'"

A dedicated wife and mother, Marlys also supported Del in other ways. In Malawi, they had a printing press whereby she would set type in the morning, then go home to make dinner and do office work. Along with caring for her family, Marlys considered her main missionary work in Malawi to be hospitality.

"We always lived in the city, and missionaries would stay with us while they came to shop or bring their children to boarding school. Also, when a new missionary family arrived, sometimes they would stay with us for two months before they found a place to live," she said. "I gave them a bed, meals, friendship, and did it all with a smile. My intention was to build team spirit as well as a family spirit. We had all left our families in the States and moved to a foreign country, and this was the only family we had."

During their time abroad, the couple witnessed God's miraculous protection and intervention on several occasions. They survived deadly bee stings and lived through a plane crash. Once, God blinded the eyes of a gang called *Young Pioneers* who stopped their vehicle in desolate northern Malawi and inspected everything, including the trunk, where there were three guns visible. The gang did not see the firearms, however, and gave the family permission to continue driving toward the Tanzania-Malawi border.

Upon returning home from Africa, Del and Marlys continued to work until Del passed away in 1997. After his death, although she missed him, she continued to find new purpose.

"When my husband died, a granddaughter who was living nearby was starting her family of six children. I decided to become her Mother's Helper. When your mate dies, you have to live for the living. Why should I give up when I have all of this life to live?" she said.

Marlys' perspective on life is so inspiring to me. When I asked what she would hope is her reputation or what she values most in life, she told me, "Beyond a doubt, being faithful to God and doing his will. A sense of humor doesn't hurt either. I am just a little old lady who has lived an extraordinary life. What's more important than loving God and doing his will?"

# REFLECT AND RESPOND

Marlys took her responsibility as a mother and invested into it. She saw the need to create "family" for others and offered it. Later on, she found someone to invest into after her husband's passing. Oftentimes, we can doubt the significance of the tasks at hand. God, however, gives us opportunities to use our abilities to work for him each and every day. It's how we choose to respond that really matters. What roles, tasks, or people have you been called to invest in now?

_____

_____

_____

_____

Who or what has God placed in front of you today?

_____

_____

_____

_____

# MY FAVORITE STORYTELLER

## Kendra Roehl

*"So here's what I want you to do, God helping you: Take your everyday, ordinary life—your sleeping, eating, going-to-work, and walking-around life—and place it before God as an offering. Embracing what God does for you is the best thing you can do for him."*

Romans 12:1-2 (MSG)

Standing in the schoolyard, I'd wait. Attending a small Christian school as a child had its perks, one of them being that it ended about the time my Uncle Jim would get off the day shift at the paper mill.

I would wait outside, hoping he'd show up while my friends were there. I was so proud of my Uncle Jim, whose exuberant personality and booming voice loomed larger than life over my shy, quiet self.

When his Ford truck would pull into the dusty drive, I'd climb up in the passenger seat beside him. We'd head out on the open road, windows down, wind in my hair. When a song came on that he liked, he'd turn up the radio, slip his hat to the side, and sing loudly with a country twang. And me? I'd be grinning from ear to ear.

We'd make a quick stop in Hill City for a can of pop and candy bar that I didn't have to share (a huge treat for this little girl, who usually had to split treats three ways with her sisters) before making our way to my uncle and aunt's farm.

He had a love for life and for people, especially kids, like few others my little eyes had seen. While most adults would engage us children for a while and then tire of our childishness, Jimmy was different. He was always glad to see us, seemingly never tired of the silliness of being a kid.

He loved people. And he loved stories.

# The story is what lives on.

In fact, few people could tell stories like my Uncle Jim. In the evenings after the work had been done, we'd sit around the table and he'd tell tales. His voice usually started off quiet, getting more animated and boisterous as the story went on. Sitting on the edge of your seat, you never knew how his story would end. Most nights he'd have us laughing so hard we'd cry. There was no need for TV with Jimmy around. His stories were entertainment enough, and I loved every one of them. Talking about the seemingly insignificant, they were stories about everyday life, songs about ketchup and mustard.

Even as an adult, I loved hearing Jim's stories. Many I had heard time and again over the years. Stories from when he was younger; many about his wife, my aunt Delpha, whom he lovingly referred to as "Girlie." It didn't matter how often I heard a story, he could always make me laugh.

*Tell me again, Jim, about the time Girlie mistakenly took men bending over in a ditch for pigs. Or the time Jeremy climbed near to the top of the pine tree out front. How about when the horses spooked and you had to sit all the way back on the hay wagon to get them to stop running.*

Reminiscing never got old.

And as it has been a little over two years since my uncle passed away, I find it is his stories I miss the most.

Sitting with my aunt, she now picks up where he left off. Telling me about their life on the farm, how they moved there so many years ago, to just a little house with no electricity or running water. Raising children, fostering and adopting others. The joys and struggles they shared together over fifty years of building a life together on the farm.

I love their story, because it is part of my story. It is flawed and beautiful, tragic yet lovely. Uncle Jim taught me that when everything else is gone, when seasons change and people pass away, the story is what lives on.

# REFLECT AND RESPOND

How have the stories of your family helped define what you believe about your own story?

_____

_____

_____

_____

How might God use the story of your family to impact those around you?

_____

_____

_____

_____